EXAM PREPARATORY MANUAL OF GYNAECOLOGY

AUTHOR

NISHANT BHUSHAN

REVIEWED BY

DR. AMUTHA (M.B.B.S , DGO , MD)

ABOUT THE AUTHOR

NISHANT BHUSHAN LIVES IN JAMSHEDPUR AND COMPLETED HIS 10TH FROM DAV BISTUPUR, FURTHER HE WENT TO SRI CHAITANIYA VIZAG FOR HIS HIGHER SECONDARY BOARDS AND FINALLY STARTED HIS JOURNEY BY PURSUING M.B.B.S FROM SRI LAKSHMI NARAYANA INSTITUTE OF MEDICAL SCIENCE PONDICHERRY.

FOR MORE DETAILS PLEASE VISIT OUR WEBSITE

www.nishantbhushan.in

SPECIAL THANKS TO...

DR. AMUTHA

(M.B.B.S , DGO , MD)

Words are powerless to express my gratitude to you mam. I thank you from the bottom of my heart for never letting me down. My gratitude to you for all you have done, which i will never forget. I truly appreciate you and your time you spent helping me in writing this book .

HEAD OF THE DEPARTMENT

OBG, SLIMS PONDY

REFERENCE

- ANATOMY - DC DUTTA'S TEXTBOOK OF GYNECOLOGY
- SHAW'S TEXTBOOK OF GYNECOLOGY
- LECTURES OF DR. SAKSHI ARORA
- LECTURES OF DR. PRASSAN VIJ
- WILLIAMS GYNECOLOGY

THIS IS NOT A TEXTBOOK BUT AN EXAM PREPARATORY MANUAL OR NOTES FOR RAPID REVISION.

CONTENTS WRITTEN IN THIS BOOK ARE FROM STANDARD TEXTBOOK. STUDENTS READING FIRST TIME ARE REQUESTED TO READ STANDARD TEXTBOOK FIRST AND THEN AT LAST MOMENTS FOR REVISION PURPOSE U CAN FOLLOW THIS BOOK.

CONTENTS

CHAPTER 1

ANATOMY

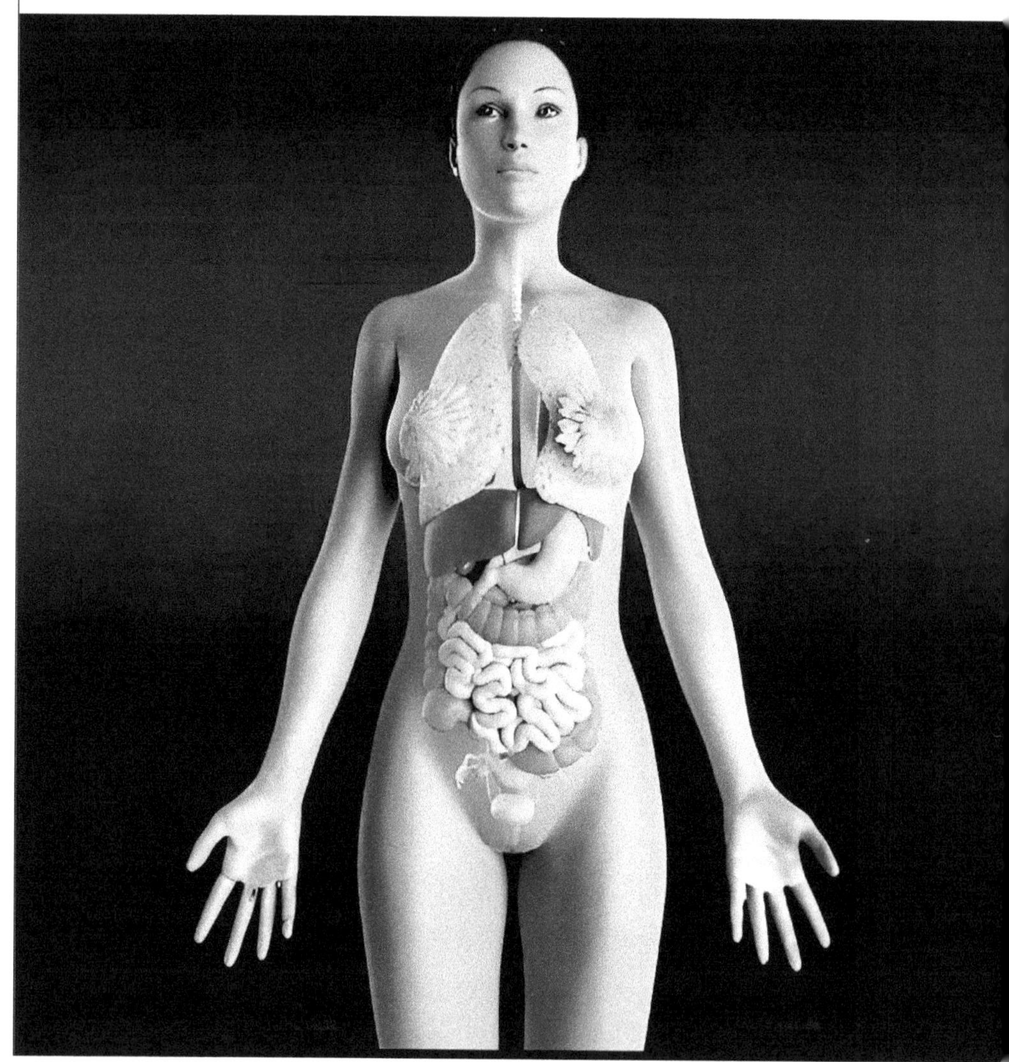

UTERUS

Uterus is a hollow pyriform muscular organ situated in the pelvis between the bladder in front and the rectum behind. position: Its normal position is one of the anteversion and anteflexion. The uterus usually inclines to the right (dextrorotation) so that the cervix is directed to the left (levorotation) and comes in close relation with the left ureter. measurements and parts: The uterus measures about 8 cm long, 5 cm wide at the fundus and its walls are about 1.25 cm thick. Its weight varies from 50–80 g. It has got the following parts.

- ✓ Body
- ✓ Isthmus
- ✓ Cervix

Body : The body is further divided into fundus—the part which lies above the openings of the uterine tubes. The body properly is triangular and lies between the openings of the tubes and the isthmus. The superolateral angles of the body of the uterus project outwards from the junction of the fundus and body and are called the cornua of the uterus. The uterine tube, round ligament, and ligament of the ovary are attached to each cornu.

Isthmus: The isthmus is a constricted part measuring about 0.5 cm situated between the body and the cervix. It is limited above by the anatomical internal os and below by the histological internal os (Aschoff). Some consider isthmus as a part of the lower portion of the body of the uterus.

Cervix: The cervix is the lowermost part of the uterus. It extends from the histological internal os and ends at external os which opens into the vagina after perforating the anterior vaginal wall. It is almost cylindrical in shape and measures about 2.5 cm in length and diameter. It is divided into a supravaginal part—the part lying above the vagina and a vaginal part which lies within the vagina, each measuring 1.25 cm. In nulliparous, the vaginal part of the cervix is conical with the external os looking circular, whereas in parous, it is cylindrical with the external os having bilateral slits. The slit is due to invariable tear of the circular muscles surrounding the external os and gives rise to anterior and posterior lips of the cervix.

Relations

Anteriorly: Above the internal os, the body forms the posterior wall of the uterovesical pouch. Below the internal os, it is separated from the base of the bladder by loose areolar tissue.

Posteriorly: It is covered by peritoneum and forms the anterior wall of the pouch of Douglas containing coils of intestine.

Laterally: The double folds of peritoneum of the broad ligament are attached laterally between which the uterine artery ascends up. Attachment of the Mackenrodt's ligament extends from the internal os down to the supravaginal cervix and lateral vaginal wall. About 1.5 cm away at the level of internal os, a little nearer on the left side is the crossing of the uterine artery and the ureter. **The uterine artery crosses from above and in front of the ureter**, soon before the ureter enters the ureteric tunnel.

VAGINA

It is a fibromusculomembranous sheath communicating the uterine cavity with the exterior at the vulva. It constitutes the excretory channel for the uterine secretion and menstrual blood. It is the organ of copulation and forms the birth canal of parturition. The canal is directed upwards and backwards forming an angle of 45° with the horizontal in erect posture. The long axis of the vagina almost lies parallel to the plane of the pelvic inlet and at right angles to that of the uterus. The diameter of the canal is about 2.5 cm, being widest in the upper part and narrowest at its introitus. It has got enough power of distensibility as evident during childbirth.

Walls: Vagina has got an anterior, a posterior, and two lateral walls. The anterior and posterior walls are placed together but the lateral walls are comparatively stiffer especially at its middle, as such it looks 'H' shaped on transverse section. The length of the anterior wall is about 7 cm and that of the posterior wall is about 9 cm .The upper end of vaginal is above the pelvic floor.

Relations

Anterior

The upper one-third is related with base of the bladder and the lower two-thirds are with the urethra, the lower half of which is firmly embedded with its wall.

Posterior

The upper one-third is related with the pouch of Douglas, the middle-third with the anterior rectal wall separated by rectovaginal septum, and the lower-third is separated from the anal canal by the perineal body .

Lateral walls

The upper one-third is related with the pelvic cellular tissue at the base of broad ligament in which the ureter and the uterine artery lie approximately 2 cm from the lateral fornices.

The middle-third is blended with the levator ani and the lower-third is related with the bulbocavernosus muscles, vestibular bulbs, and Bartholin's glands.

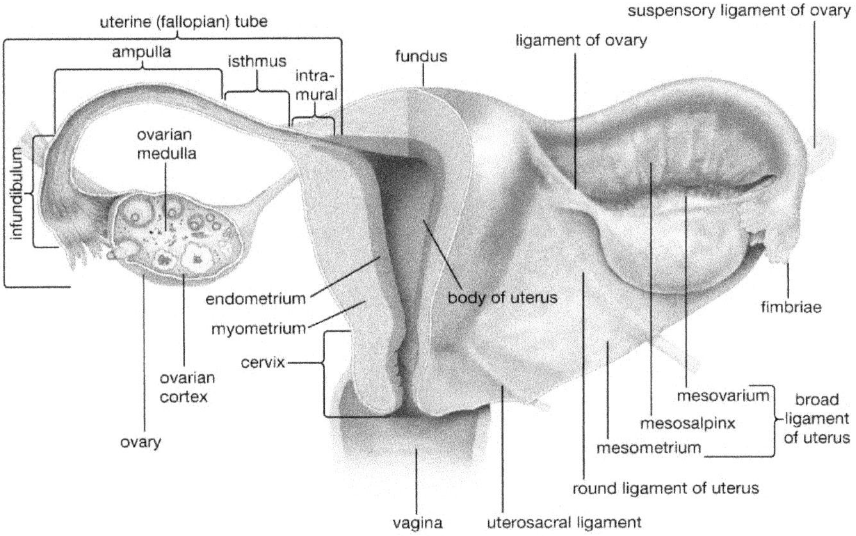

Neurovasculature

It is supplied by branches of the uterine arteries (branch of the internal iliac artery). One branch travels within the broad ligament of the uterus until the region close to the ovarian hilum, where it forms an anastomosis with the uterine branches of the ovarian artery (branch of the abdominal aorta). The second branch supplies the cervix and anastomoses with several branches of the vaginal artery. The uterine artery also gives several perforating branches within the uterine wall that form two surrounding systems around the uterus called the posterior and anterior arcuate arteries. The venous blood drains through the uterine venous plexus into the internal iliac vein.

The nerve supply of the uterus is derived principally from the sympathetic system and partly from the parasympathetic system. Sympathetic components are from T5 and T6 (motor) and T10 to L1 spinal segments (sensory). The somatic distribution of uterine pain is that area of the abdomen supplied by T10 to L1. The parasympathetic system is represented on either side by the pelvic nerve which consists of both motor and sensory fibers from S2, S3, S4 and ends in the ganglia of Frankenhauser which lies on either sides of the cervix.

Lymphatics

Lymphatic vessels drain lymph from the body and cervix of the uterus to the iliac lymph nodes (external and internal), as well as the obturator lymph nodes. In turn, the fundus is drained to the para-aortic lymph nodes.

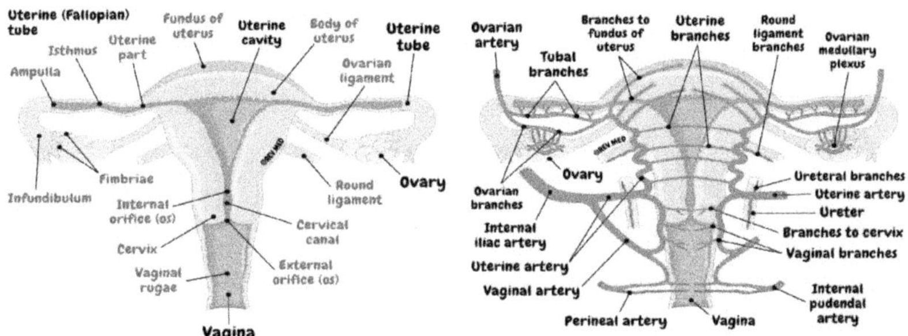
The Uterus
NORMAL STRUCTURE
Uterine (Fallopian) tube
Fundus of uterus
Uterine cavity
Body of uterus
Uterine tube
Isthmus
Uterine part
Ampulla
Ovarian ligament
Fimbriae
Infundibulum
Internal orifice (os)
Round ligament
Ovary
Cervical canal
Cervix
Vaginal rugae
External orifice (os)
Vagina
The Uterus
BLOOD SUPPLY
Ovarian artery
Branches to fundus of uterus
Uterine branches
Round ligament branches
Ovarian medullary plexus
Tubal branches
Ovary
Ureteral branches
Ovarian branches
Uterine artery
Ureter
Internal iliac artery
Branches to cervix
Vaginal branches
Uterine artery
Vaginal artery
Internal pudendal artery
Perineal artery
Vagina

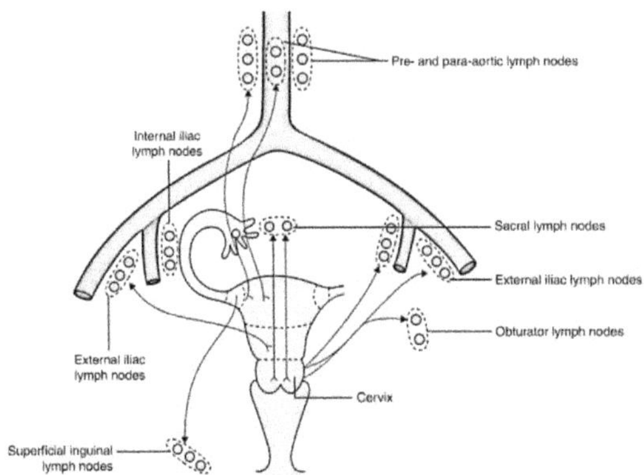
Pre- and para-aortic lymph nodes
Internal iliac lymph nodes
Sacral lymph nodes
External iliac lymph nodes
Obturator lymph nodes
External iliac lymph nodes
Cervix
Superficial inguinal lymph nodes

Histology of the uterus

The uterus has three layers: mucosa (endometrium), muscularis (myometrium) and serosa/adventitia (perimetrium).

The endometrium (uterine mucous membrane) is lined with simple columnar epithelium (lamina epithelialis) and contains numerous tubular glands. It is followed by a cell-rich connective tissue layer (lamina propria). There is a transition to squamous non-keratinized epithelium at the portio (squamocolumnar junction). Physiologically the endometrium is divided into the functional layer (stratum functionale) and basal layer (stratum basale).

- The myometrium (uterine musculature) comprises a complex of three smooth muscle layers which are microscopically difficult to separate (from the inside to the outside):
    - The subvascular layer is rather thin and mainly participates in the sealing of the tubes and the separation of the endometrium during the menstrual cycle.
    - The vascular layer is quite strong and well-perfused running around the uterus like a net. It plays a major role during labor.
    - The supravascular layer is again a thin sheet of crossing muscle fibers stabilizing the uterine wall.
- The perimetrium equals the peritoneum and is surrounded by a thin connective tissue layer (Tela subserosa). In peritoneal free areas there is no serosa but adventitia.

Function

The uterus plays an important role in human reproduction. It is the organ where the implantation and nourishment of the fertilized ovum takes place. Furthermore it helps pushing out the baby during birth through muscle contraction.

The uteruses of women in childbearing age underlie an about 28-day hormone-controlled rhythm (menstrual cycle) which goes through three phases:

- During the menstrual phase (day 1 to 4) the spiral arteries in the endometrium contract leading to an ischemia and sloughing of the functional layer (desquamation). At the same time coagulation factors in the menstrual blood are decomposed in order to avoid blood clotting. This phase is predominately controlled by estrogen causing painful contractions of the uterine musculature. A total blood loss during this phase is about 80ml; more than that is considered abnomal (menorrhagia).

- During the proliferative phase (day 5 to 14) the cells of the basal layer divide rapidly leading to a fast regeneration of the epithelium, functional layer and spiral arteries.
- The secretory phase (day 15 to 28) begins with the ovulation stopping the proliferation and preparing an implantation of the ovum. It comes to an intracellular accumulation of glycogen and a dilatation of the uterine lumen. The glands have a saw-tooth-like shape and increasingly secrete nutrients. The endometrial stromal cells resemble the decidua of the placenta (predecidual cells). The spiral arteries are triggered to supply a possible placenta. If no fertilization occurs during the secretory phase the spiral arteries contract and the cycle begins again.

SUPPORT OF UTERUS

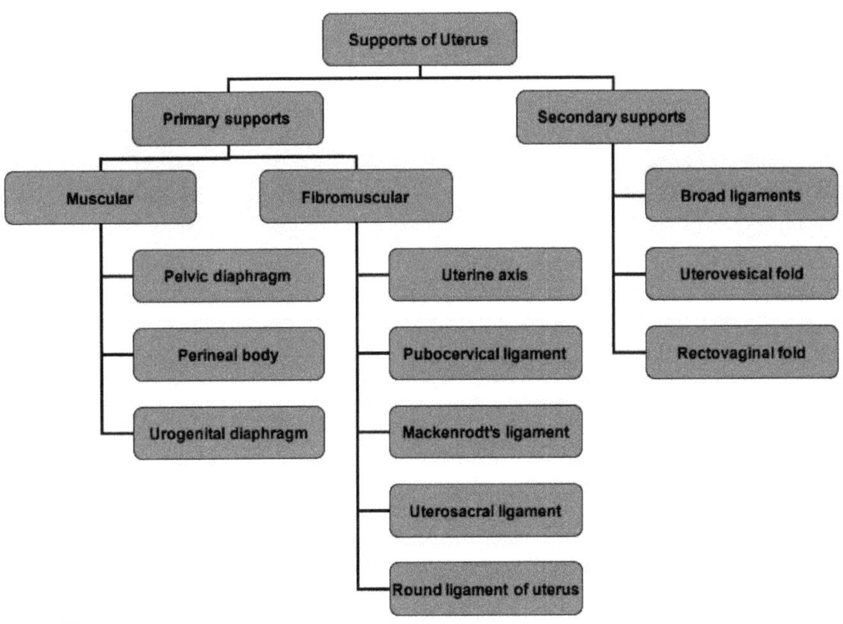

CHAPTER 2

MULLERIAN DUCT ANOMALIES

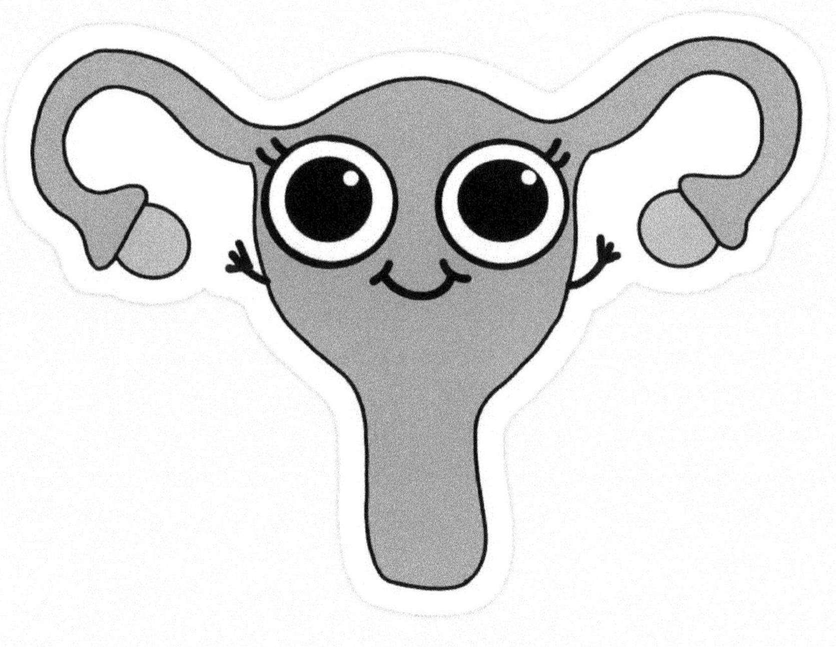

Müllerian duct anomalies are those structural anomalies caused by errors in müllerian-duct development during embryonic morphogenesis.

Defects are as follows:-

- Arrested development
- Fusion defects vertical / lateral
- Failure of resorption of septum

Cryptomenorrhea

It is a occurrence of menstrual symptoms without external bleeding as menstrual blood fails to come out from genital tract due to obstruction in the outflow passage.

Causes :

Congenital

- ✓ Imperforate hymen
- ✓ Transverse vaginal septum

Acquired

- ✓ Amputation
- ✓ Cauterization
- ✓ Conization

Symptoms

- Normal secondary sexual characterstics complaints of primary amenorrhea
- h/o cyclical abdominal pain is present

Treatment

Drainage of blood (cruciate incision)

MULLERIAN AGENESIS

Absence of mullarian duct , so the structure formed by mullerian duct are absent .

Structure which all are absents are as follows

- fallopian tube
- uterus
- cervix
- upper vagina

Karyotype – 44XX

- ✓ Gonads normal as it develops from genital ridge
  So ovary will be normal so ovulation will also be normal in these patients , every thing will be normal but they will complaint of ammenorrhoea due to absence of uterus.

Diagnosis

Karyotyping

Mx

- ➢ Uterus absent so we cant initiate mensturation
- ➢ Coital difficulty (as upper vagina is absent)
  So we can treat this by vaginoplasty
- ➢ Female cant be pregnant but can have own biological child (as have ovulation)
  So we can do IVF + SURROGACY

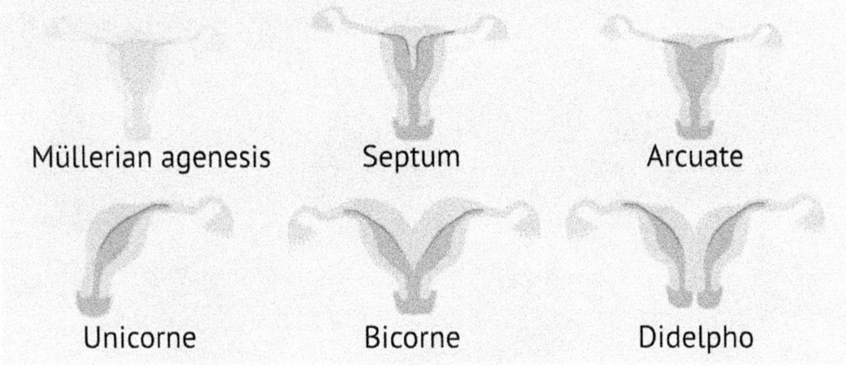

IMPERFORATE HYMEN

This is when the hymen covers the entire vaginal area with no openings at all. This type is usually detected at an early age, as it causes a constant abdominal pain, and it usually requires a surgical treatment. Due to its nature, menstrual blood can't flow out which causes that pain, and that's why that case needs a medical examination.

- It is actually not a mullerian anomaly
- It is a cannulation defect
- In this hymen didn't formed properly so menstruation blood accumulate inside vagina and uterus.

It is most often diagnosed in adolescent girls when menstrual blood accumulates in the vagina and sometimes also in the uterus. It is treated by surgical incision of the hymen.

Signs And Symptoms

- In newborns may present with acute urinary retention.
- In adolescent,the most common symptoms are cyclic pelvic pain and amenorrhea, other symptoms associated with - hematocolpos(a medical condition in which the vagina fills with menstrual blood) include urinary retention, constipation, back pain, nausea, and diarrhea.

Management

Before surgical intervention in adolescents, symptoms can be relieved by the combined oral contraceptive pill taken continuously to suppress the menstrual cycle or NSAIDsto relieve pain.

Surgical treatment of the imperforate hymen by hymenotomy(removal or opening of the hymen)

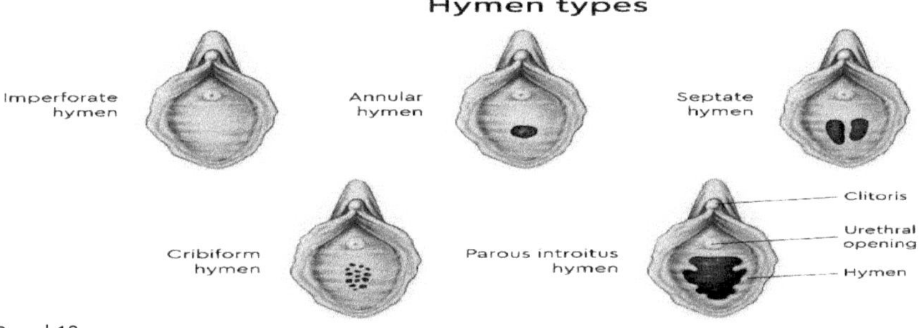

CHAPTER 3

MENSTRUAL CYCLE

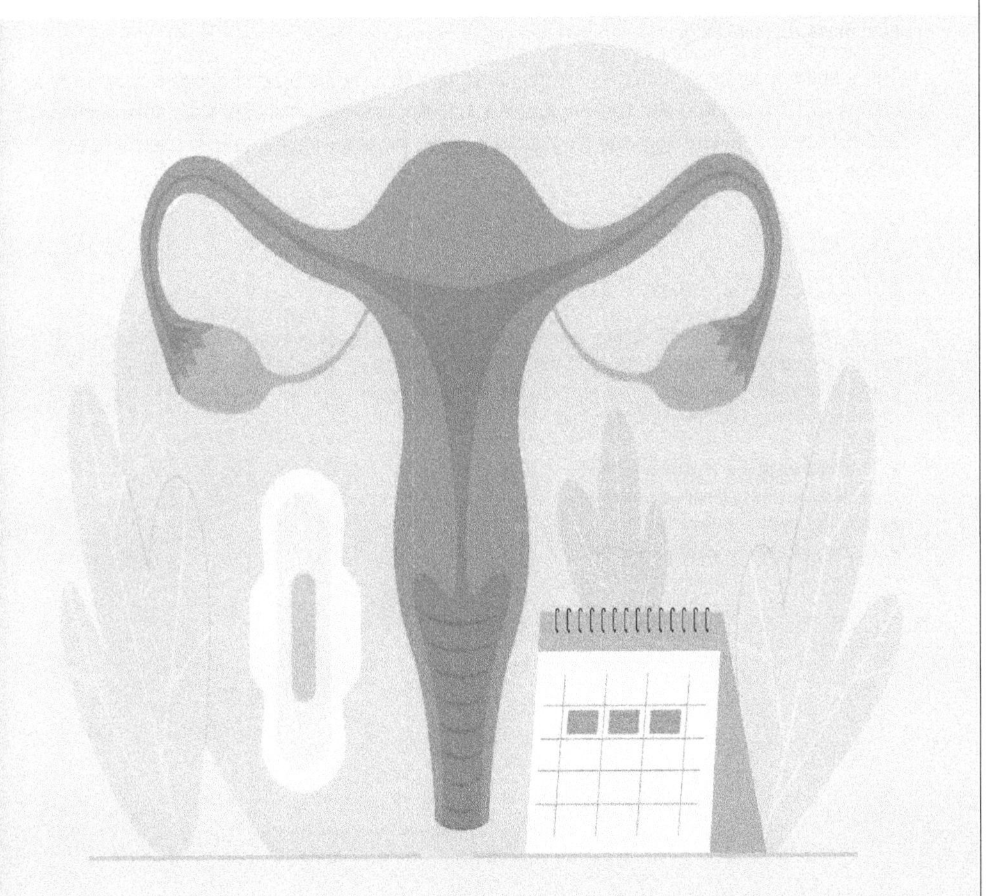

What is a menstrual cycle?

The menstrual cycle is the process by which a woman's body prepares for pregnancy. Once a month, the female body grows a new uterine lining (endometrium) that is ready to receive and nourish a fertilized egg. If an egg is not fertilized, the uterus sheds the endometrium and a woman experiences menstrual bleeding, or her period.

Most women have their first period, or menarche, between the ages of 11-14 and have regular menstrual cycles until about age 50. The menstrual cycle typically lasts about 28 days; however, it is normal to have a cycle that is a few days shorter or longer.

The days of a menstrual cycle are counted from Day 1 of menstrual bleeding to Day 1 of the next menstrual bleeding.

The menstrual cycle is guided by hormonal signals sent by the brain. Estrogen causes the uterine lining to develop and thicken; follicle-stimulating hormone stimulates the development and release of a mature egg; and progesterone levels increase in order to help a fertilized egg attach to the uterine lining.

Phases of Menstrual cycle

The day count for menstrual cycle begins on the first day of menstruation when blood starts to come out of the vagina. In this section, the length of menstrual cycle has been assumed to be 28 days (which is the average among women). The entire duration of a Menstrual cycle can be divided into four main phases:

1. **Menstrual phase (From day 1 to 5)**
2. **Follicular phase (From day 1 to 13)**
3. **Ovulation phase (Day 14)**
4. **Luteal phase (From day 15 to 28)**

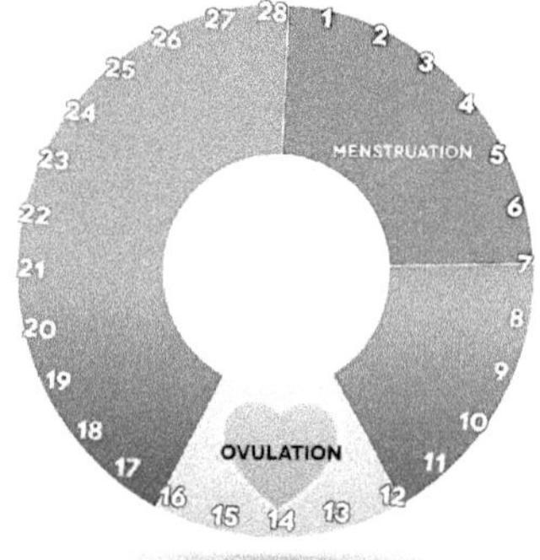

Menstrual phase (day 1-5)

Menstrual phase begins on the first day of menstruation and lasts till the 5th day of the menstrual cycle. The following events occur during this phase:

- The uterus sheds its inner lining of soft tissue and blood vessels which exits the body from the vagina in the form of menstrual fluid.
- Blood loss of 10 ml to 80 ml is considered normal.
- You may experience abdominal cramps. These cramps are caused by the contraction of the uterine and the abdominal muscles to expel the menstrual fluid.

Follicular phase (day 1-13)

This phase also begins on the first day of menstruation, but it lasts till the 13th day of the menstrual cycle. The following events occur during this phase:

- The pituitary gland secretes a hormone that stimulates the egg cells in the ovaries to grow.
- One of these egg cells begins to mature in a sac-like-structure called follicle. It takes 13 days for the egg cell to reach maturity.
- While the egg cell matures, its follicle secretes a hormone that stimulates the uterus to develop a lining of blood vessels and soft tissue called endometrium.

Ovulation phase (day 14)

On the 14th day of the cycle, the pituitary gland secretes a hormone that causes the ovary to release the matured egg cell. The released egg cell is swept into the fallopian tube by the cilia of the fimbriae. Fimbriae are finger like projections located at the end of the fallopian tube close to the ovaries and cilia are slender hair like projections on each Fimbria.

Luteal phase (day 15-28)

This phase begins on the 15th day and lasts till the end of the cycle. The following events occur during this phase:

- The egg cell released during the ovulation phase stays in the fallopian tube for 24 hours.

- If a sperm cell does not impregnate the egg cell within that time, the egg cell disintegrates.
- The hormone that causes the uterus to retain its endometrium gets used up by the end of the menstrual cycle. This causes the menstrual phase of the next cycle to begin.

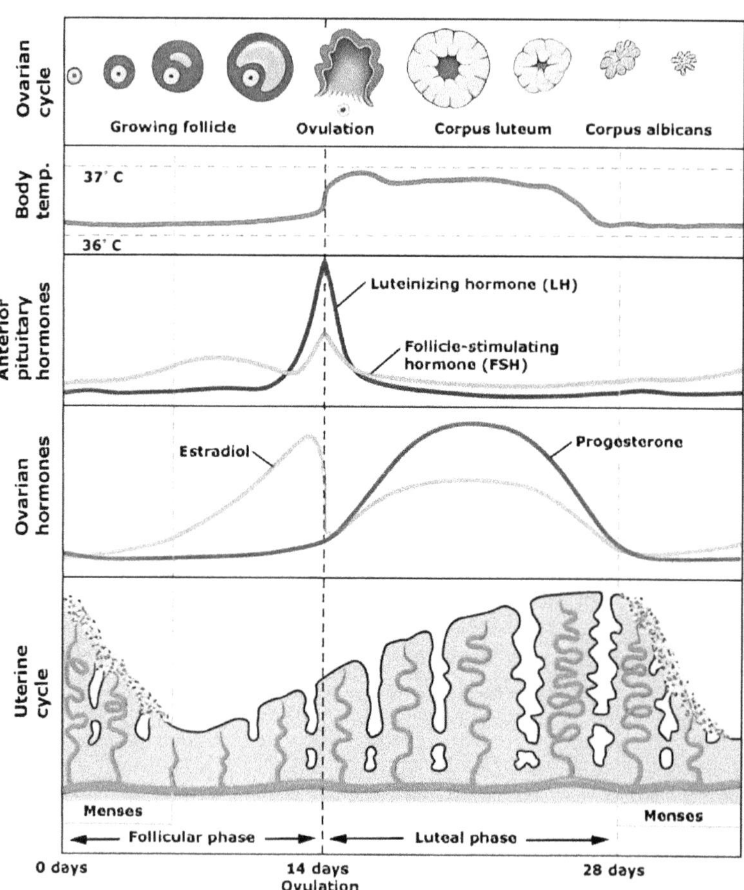

CHAPTER - 4

BLEEDING DISORDERS

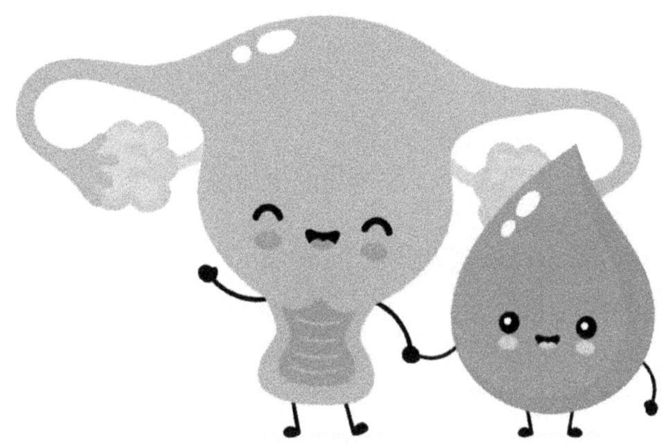

POST MENOPAUSAL BLEEDING

Bleeding occurring through vagina after the menopause (45- 50 yrs) is known as post menopausal bleeding .

Etiology

- Vulva – Trauma, vulvitis , benign & malignant lesions
- Vagina – Ring pessary , Tumor
- Cervix – Cervicitis , erosions , polyps , prolapse
- Uterus – Endometrosis , hyperplasia , endometrial carcinoma
- Fallopian tube – Malignancy
- Ovary – benign tumor , malignant tumor
- Hypertension
- Urinary tract – papilloma , carcinoma of bladder
- Bowel bleeding – rectal cancer
- HRT

Clinical Feature

- Abdominal pain
- Foul smelling discharge
- Urinary problem & rectal symptoms

Investigations

- Blood count
- Blood sugar
- Endometrial study
- Sonosalphingography
- Usg
- Vibra aspirator
- Ct scan
- Mri
- Diagnostic laproscopy
- Cystoscopy
- Proctoscopy

Management

- Once the cause is diagnosed – The treatment is based upon it
- If no cause & have minimal bleeding once or twice then observation is mandatory.
- If cases reoccur – do laparotomy & perform hysterectomy.

MENORRHAGIA

It is either excessive in amount or duration of cyclic bleeding .

Causes

- Fibroid
- Adenomyosis
- IUCD
- Tubo ovarian mass
- Tuberculosis endometritis
- Retroverted uterus
- Fibroid uterus
- Deficiency of clotting factor
- Women with anti coagulation therapy.

Investigations

- CBC
- Bleeding time
- Prothrombin time
- Cervicak cytology
- Usg
- Endometrial sampling
- Hysteroscopy

Management

- Treatment of anemia –oral iron therapy
- It include medical & surgical management

Medical management – Anti fibrinolytics
- Prostaglandin synthetase inhibitors
- Progestins orals

Surgical Management – Endometrial ablation – dimination of endometrium by resection or thermal energy
- Hysterectomy

Rest the treatment is totally based upon a cause

PUBERTY MENORRHAGIA

Excessive menstruation between menarche and 19yr of age is called puberty menorrhagia .

Etiology

- The commonest cause lie in the hypothalamic pituitary ovarian dysfunction
- Hypothyroidism
- PCOD
- Genital TB
- Liver disorder

Clinical features

- Normal bleeding last for several days
- Anemia

Investigations

- Blood profile
- X-ray chest for TB
- Thyroid function test
- Pelvic ultrasound

Management

- ✓ Control menorrhagia
- ✓ Prevent or treat anemia
- ✓ Prevent recurrence
- ✓ Treat the cause

DYSMENORRHEA

It is defined as a painful menstruation.

Types

- Primary / spasmodic – It mostly occurs after a few years of menarche.(In absence of any pelvic pathology.)
- Secondary / congestive – It is said to be associated with pelvic pathology and mostly occurs after few years of menarche .

Common cause

- Endometriosis
- Adenomyosis
- IUCD
- Cervical stenosis

Investigations

- Pelvic sonography
- CT scan

- MRI
- Blood profile

Treatment

- ✓ Analgesics
- ✓ Antispasmotic
- ✓ Nsaids

DYSFUNCTIONAL UTERINE BLEEDING

Dysfunctional uterine bleeding occurs when the normal cycle of menstruation is disrupted, usually due to anovulation (failure to ovulate) that's unrelated to another illness. Ovulation failure is the most common type of DUB in adolescents and in women who are reaching perimenopause.

It is of two types –

1. An-ovulatory
2. Ovulatory

In an-ovulatory DUB, estrogen is continually secreted but an egg never ripens in the follicle. Because an egg is never released, progesterone is never produced from the corpus luteum to counteract the uterine lining proliferation. Eventually the uterine lining outgrows its blood supply and sloughs off at irregular intervals. Because an egg was never produced, the premenstrual and menstrual symptoms associated with ovulation and progesterone don't occur, and the uterine bleeding is usually painless. The effects of unopposed estrogen on the uterine lining have been directly linked to endometrial hyperplasia and cancer.

Dysfunctional uterine bleeding can occur with declining estrogen levels at the end of a woman's reproductive life. Although the ovaries may still be stimulated to produce follicular ripening, they make only a very small amount of estrogen. This results in irregular shedding of the endometrium lining. Because the amount of lining proliferation is less, bleeding is usually less copious.

Ovulatory – it is a rare condition which occurs following childbirth or during adolescence & pre menopausal period.

What's AUB?

Bleeding that differs in quantity or timing from a woman's usual menstrual flow is considered AUB. For instance, a woman may bleed more heavily during one period and more lightly the next, spot between periods, or have a shorter or longer interval between periods. Some women may bleed for less than 2 days or more than 7 days.

Women who bleed heavily on a regular basis most likely have an ovulatory cycle problem rather than an an-ovulatory cycle one. Because these women are usually ovulating, they tend to experience premenstrual symptoms and cramping.

So what causes AUB? The most common causes are pregnancy and pregnancy-related conditions. The list of other causes is extensive and includes infections of the genital tract, fibroids, malignancies, medications, blood dyscrasias, and disorders of the thyroid gland, adrenal gland, kidney, or liver. Even stress can cause AUB.

Etiology

- Estrogen withdrawl
- Trauma
- Ovarian tumor
- Anovulation
- Coagulopathies
- Hormonal contraception
- Endocrine disorders
- Complication of pregnancy
- Polyps

Investigations

- TVS
- TSA
- Serum progesterone
- MRI
- Endometrial biopsy

- Hysteroscopy
- FSH & LH
- Prolactinemia

Management

1. Medical management
2. Surgical management

Medical management includes

- ✓ Progestin therapy
- ✓ Medoxy progesterone acetate
- ✓ Oral contraceptive pills
- ✓ DMPA
- ✓ NSAIDS.
- ✓ Clomiphene citrate , Cc + Hmg
- ✓ Gnrh analog
- ✓ Prednisolone

Surgical management includes

- ✓ NCl – Yag laser endometrial
- ✓ Transcervical resection of endometrium
- ✓ Hysterectomy
- ✓ Endometrial ablation
- ✓ Laparoscopic ovarian drilling

PALM- COEIN CLASSIFICATION

AUB-P (polyp) AUB-A (adenomyosis) AUB-L (leiomyoma) AUB-M (malignancy and hyperplasia)	AUB-C (coagulopathy) AUB-O (ovulatory disorders) AUB-I (iatrogenic) AUB-E (endometrial) AUB-N (not yet classified)

AMENORRHEA

It is an absence of menstrual cycle .

Types

1. Pathological
2. Physiological
3. Primary amenorrhea
4. Secondary amenorrhea

Physiological – It occur naturally prior to onset of puberty , during pregnancy & lactation & after menopause .

Pathological - It is the results of genetic factors systemic disease endocrinopathies , disturbance of the hypothalamic pituitary – ovarian uterine axis , drug usage.

Primary – It refers to the failure of onset of menstruation beyond the age of 16yr regardless of development of secondary sexual characters.

Secondary – It refers to the failure of occurrence of menstruation for 6 months or longer in women who have previously menstruated .

PRIMARY AMENORRHEA

It refers to the failure of onset of menstruation beyond the age of 16yr regardless of development of secondary sexual characters.

Causes:

The causes of primary amenorrhea are as follows:

A. Hypogonadotropic hypogonadism

1. Delayed puberty — delayed GnRH pulse reactivation.
2. Hypothalamic and pituitary dysfunction — Gonadotropin deficiency due to stress, weight loss, excessive exercise, anorexia nervosa, chronic disease (tuberculosis).

3. Kallmann's syndrome — inadequate GnRH pulse secretion — reduced FSH and LH
4. Central nervous system tumors — craniopharyngioma → reduced GnRH secretion → reduced FSH and LH.

B. Hypergonadotropic hypogonadism

1. Resistant ovarian syndrome
2. Galactosemia: Due to premature ovarian failure
3. Enzyme deficiency

C. Abnormal chromosomal pattern

1. Turner's syndrome (45 X)
2. Various mosaic states 45 X/46 XX.
3. Pure gonadal dysgenesis (46 XX or 46 XY)

D. Developmental defect of genital tract

1. Imperforate hymen
2. Transverse vaginal septum.
3. Atresia upper-third of vagina and cervix
4. Complete absence of vagina

Investigations

- Ultrasonography
- laparoscopy
- karyotype
- IVP
- Progesterone challenge test
- HSG
- Hysteroscopy
- Serum estradiol
- Serum gonadotropins
- ovarian biopsy
- Serum TSH
- T3, T4
- Blood sugar

Treatment

- Treat the cause.
- Drug-induced hyperprolactinaemia requires stoppage of drug or alternative therapy.
- Bromocriptine and long-acting derivatives are effective in most cases. Menstrual cycles are restored in 3 months time. Ninety per cent ovulate and 70–80% conceive.
- Quinagolide 25–150 mg daily in divided doses with a maintenance dose of 75 mg daily.
- The drugs are discussed in detail in the chapter on hormonal therapy.
- Macroadenoma (more than 10 mm) and microadenoma not responding to drugs require transsphenoidal adenectomy or radiotherapy 4500 cGY for 25 days.

SECONDARY AMENORRHEA

It refers to the failure of occurrence of menstruation for 6 months or longer in women who have previously menstruated.

Etiology

Uterine factors

- ✓ Tubercular endometritis
- ✓ Postradiation
- ✓ Synechiae
- ✓ Surgical removal

Ovarian factors

- ✓ Polycystic ovarian syndrome
- ✓ Premature ovarian failure
- ✓ Resistant ovarian syndrome (Savage's syndrome)
- ✓ Hyperestrogenic state

Pituitary factors

- ✓ Adenoma
- ✓ cushing's disease

- ✓ Acromegaly
- ✓ Sheehan's syndrome
- ✓ Simmond's disease

Iatrogenic

- ✓ contraceptive pills
- ✓ Psychotrophic phenothiazine derivative drugs
- ✓ Antihypertensive drugs like reserpine or dopamine antagonists

Thyroid factors

- ✓ Hypothyroid state

Adrenal factors

- ✓ Adrenal tumor or hyperplasia
- ✓ cushing syndrome

Investigations

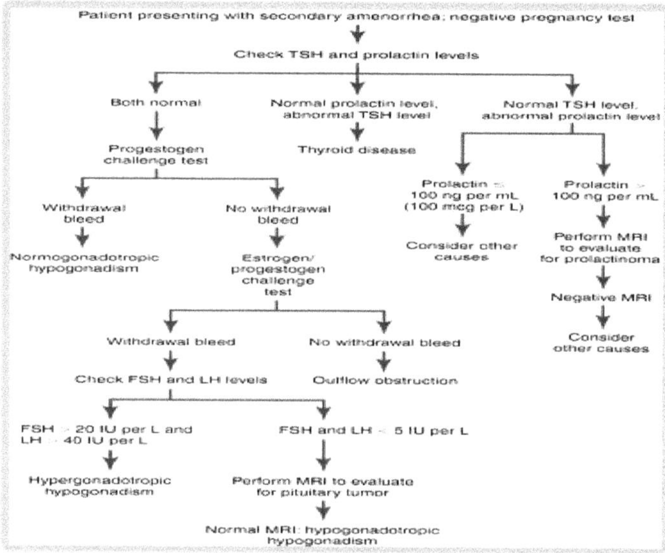

Treatment

Treat the underline cause.

CHAPTER - 5

ENDOCRINE DISORDERS

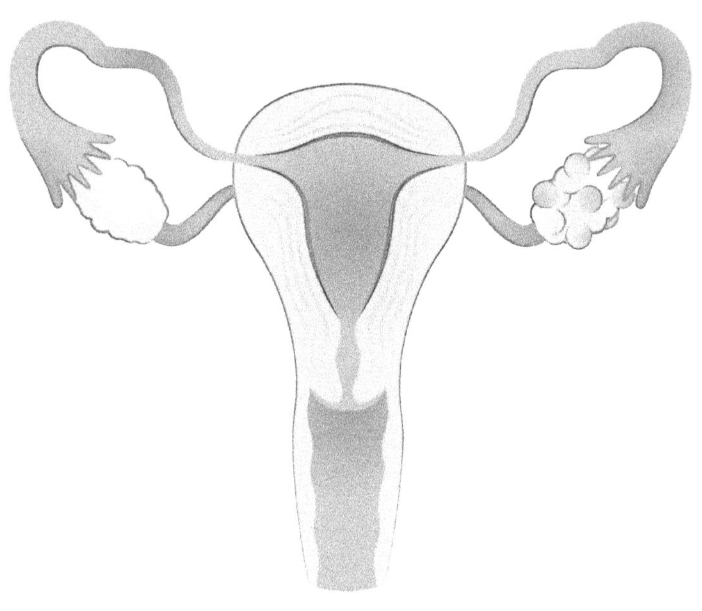

POLYCYSTIC OVARY SYNDROME

PCOS is a syndrome of ovarian dysfunction along with the cardinal features of hyperandrogenism and polycystic ovary morphology Its clinical manifestations include menstrual irregularities, signs of androgen excess (e.g. hirsutism) and obesity. Elevated serum LH levels and insulin resistance and are also common features. PCOS is associated with an increased risk of type 2 diabetes and cardiovascular events. It affects around 5–10 per cent of women of reproductive age. The prevalence of polycystic ovaries seen on ultrasound is much higher at around 25 percent

Aetiology

The aetiology of PCOS is not completely clear, but there is often a family history. It seems likely that a gene is important in its development.

Clinical features

The clinical features of PCOS are as follows:

- ✓ oligomenorrhoea/amenorrhoea in up to 75 per cent of patients, predominantly related to chronic anovulation
- ✓ hirsutism
- ✓ subfertility in up to 75 per cent of women;
- ✓ obesity in at least 40 per cent of patients;
- ✓ recurrent miscarriage in around 50–60 per cent of women
- ✓ acanthosis nigricans (areas of increased velvety skin pigmentation occur in the axillae and other flexures)
- ✓ may be asymptomatic.

Diagnosis

Patients must have two out of the three features below:

- amenorrhoea/oligomenorrhoea;

- clinical or biochemical hyperandrogenism;
- polycystic ovaries on ultrasound.

The ultrasound criteria for the diagnosis of a polycystic ovary are eight or more subcapsular follicular cysts <10 mm in diameter and increased ovarian stroma.

While these findings support a diagnosis of PCOS,they are not by themselves sufficient to identify the syndrome.

Management

Management of PCOS involves the following:

- ✓ COCP: This should regulate menstruation.
- ✓ Cyclical oral progesterone: This too can be used to regulate menstruation.
- ✓ Metformin: This is beneficial in a subset of patients with PCOS, those with hyperinsulinaemia and cardiovascular risk factors. It is less effective than clomiphene for ovulation induction and it does not improve pregnancy outcome. It should be discontinued when pregnancy is detected.
- ✓ Clomiphene: This can be used to induce ovulation where subfertility is a factor.
- ✓ Lifestyle advice: Dietary modification and exercise is appropriate in these patients as they are at an increased risk of developing diabetes and cardiovascular disease later in life.
- ✓ Weight reduction.

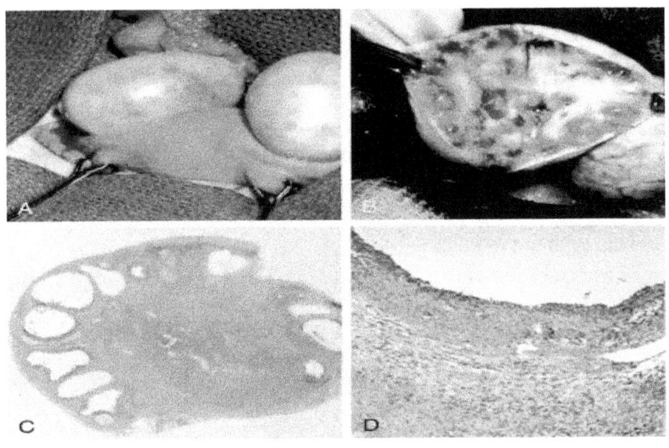
A
B
C
D

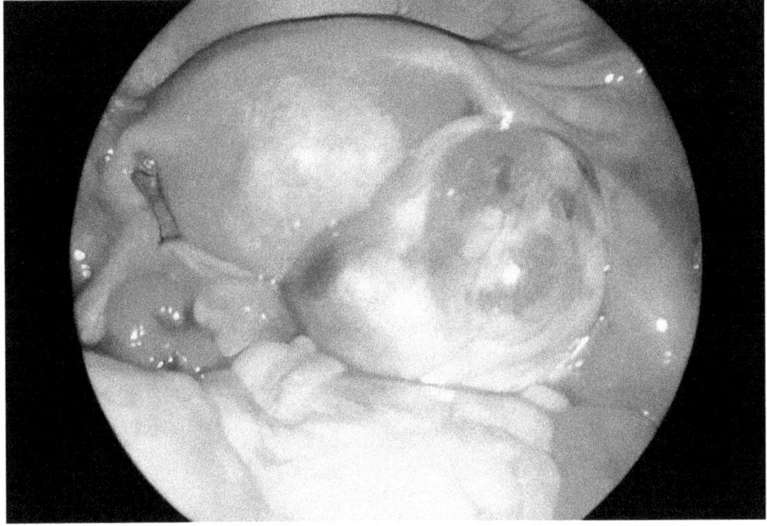

HIRSUTISM

Hirsutism is the excessive growth of androgen dependent sexual hair in facial and central part of the body.

Causes

- **Ovarian**
  - ✓ Polycystic ovarian syndrome
  - ✓ Sertoli-Leydig cell tumor
  - ✓ Hilus cell tumor
  - ✓ Lipoid cell tumor
  - ✓ Hyperthecosis – Luteoma of pregnancy
- **Adrenal**
  - ✓ Adrenal hyperplasia (congenital or late onset)
  - ✓ Cushing's syndrome
  - ✓ Adrenal tumor
- **Obesity**
  - ✓ Insulin resistance and androgen excess
  - ✓ HAIR–AN syndrome
- **Exogenous** (drug therapy)
  - ✓ Androgens, anabolics, oral contraceptives, synthetic progestogens, danazol, phenytoin, diazoxide, cortisone, etc.
- **Post-menopause**
- **Pituitary tumor**
  - ✓ secreting excess ACTH (Cushing's diseases)
  - ✓ Excess growth hormone (acromegaly)
- **Idiopathic:**
  - ✓ Increased sensitivity to androgens

Treatment

- Eflornithine cream applied topically;
- Cyproterone acetate (anti-androgen contraceptive pill)
- Metformin: improves parameters of insulin resistance, hyperandrogenemia, anovulation and acne in PCOS;
- GnRH analogues with low-dose HRT: this regime should be reserved for women intolerant of other therapies;
- Surgical treatments, e.g. laser or electrolysis

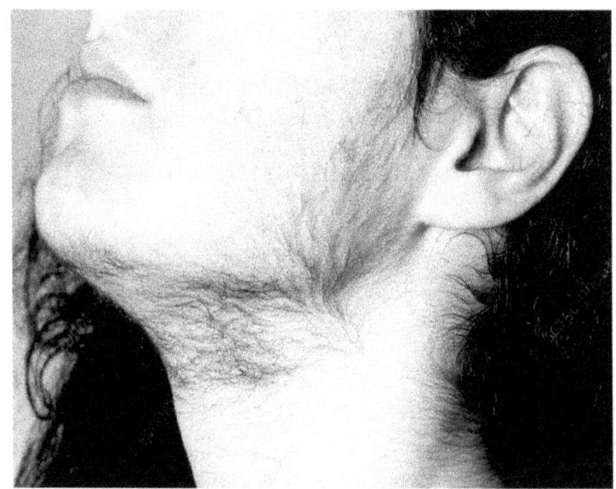

Turner syndrome

- A chromosomal disorder in which a female is born with only one X chromosome.
- 45X & 45XO

Types

Monosomy X: Each cell has only one X chromosome instead of two. About 45% of people with TS have this type. It comes from the mother's egg or the father's sperm randomly forming without an X chromosome. After fertilization, the baby's cells also contain this defect.

Mosaic Turner syndrome: Also called 45,X mosaicism, this type makes up about 30% of Turner syndrome cases. Some of the baby's cells have a pair of X chromosomes, while other cells only have one. It happens randomly during cell division early in pregnancy.

Inherited Turner syndrome: In rare cases, babies may have inherited TS, meaning their parent (or parents) were born with it and passed it on. This type usually happens because of a missing part of the X chromosome.

Symptoms

- Wide or weblike neck
- Low-set ears
- Broad chest with widely spaced nipples
- High, narrow roof of the mouth (palate)
- Arms that turn outward at the elbows
- Fingernails and toenails that are narrow and turned upward
- Swelling of the hands and feet, especially at birth
- Slightly smaller than average height at birth
- Slowed growth
- Cardiac defects
- Low hairline at the back of the head
- Receding or small lower jaw
- Short fingers and toes

Complications

Turner syndrome can affect the proper development of several body systems, but this varies greatly among individuals with the syndrome. Complications that can occur include:

- **Heart problems.** Many infants with Turner syndrome are born with heart defects or even slight abnormalities in heart structure that increase their risk of serious complications. Heart defects often include problems with the aorta, the large blood vessel that branches off the heart and delivers oxygen-rich blood to the body.
- **High blood pressure**. Turner syndrome can increase the risk of high blood pressure — a condition that increases the risk of developing diseases of the heart and blood vessels.
- **Hearing loss.** Hearing loss is common with Turner syndrome. In some cases, this is due to the gradual loss of nerve function. An increased risk of frequent middle ear infections can also result in hearing loss.
- **Vision problems.** An increased risk of weak muscle control of eye movements (strabismus), nearsightedness and other vision problems can occur with Turner syndrome.
- **Kidney problems**. Turner syndrome may be associated with malformations of the kidneys. Although these abnormalities generally don't cause medical problems, they may increase the risk of urinary tract infections.
- **Autoimmune disorders.** Turner syndrome can increase the risk of an underactive thyroid (hypothyroidism) due to the autoimmune disorder Hashimoto's thyroiditis. There is also an increased risk of diabetes. Sometimes Turner syndrome is associated with gluten intolerance (celiac disease) or inflammatory bowel disease.
- **Skeletal problems.** Problems with the growth and development of bones increase the risk of abnormal curvature of the spine (scoliosis) and forward rounding of the upper back (kyphosis). Turner syndrome can also increase the risk of developing weak, brittle bones (osteoporosis).
- **Learning disabilities**. Girls and women with Turner syndrome usually have normal intelligence. However, there is increased risk of learning disabilities, particularly with learning that involves spatial concepts, math, memory and attention.
- **Mental health issues.** Girls and women with Turner syndrome may have challenges functioning in social situations, may experience anxiety and depression, and may have an increased risk of attention-deficit/hyperactivity disorder (ADHD).
- **Infertility.** Most females with Turner syndrome are infertile. However, a very small number may become pregnant spontaneously, and some can become pregnant with fertility treatment.

- **Pregnancy complications.** Because women with Turner syndrome are at increased risk of complications during pregnancy, such as high blood pressure and aortic dissection.

Investigations:

- Sex chromatin study is negative.
- Karyotype is 45, XO.
- Serum E2 is very low.
- Serum FSH and LH are elevated.
- Autoantibodies may be present
- Amniocentesis and chorionic villous sampling

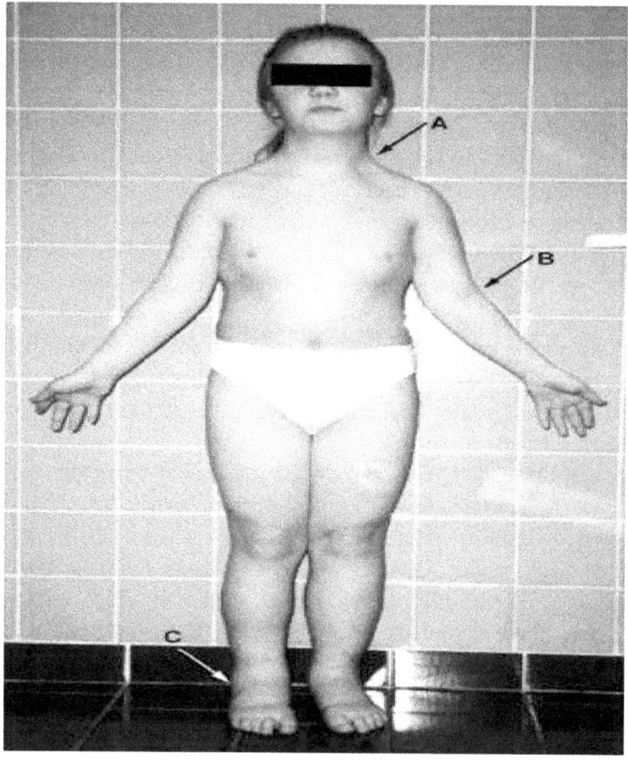

CHAPTER - 6

BENIGN LESIONS

FIBROID

- It is the most common benign tumor in females.
- It is estrogen and progesterone dependent tumor.
- Most common age group affected is 35-45 yrs.
- It is mostly seen in nulliparous women.

Etiology

- 50 yrs old women 80% of chances
- Chromosomal abnormality
    - 12-14 translocation
    - 12 trisomy
    - 7 deletion
- Obese women
- Red meat eater
- Nulliparous women
- Estrogen & progesterones
- Family history
- Early menarche

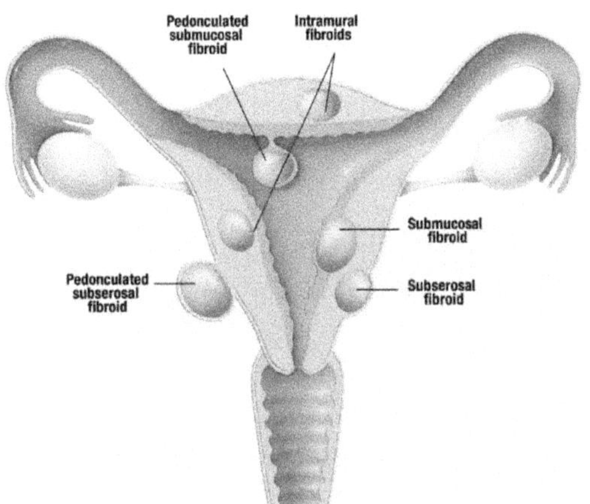

Classification

- Intramural
- Submucosal
- Subserosal

Protective factors :

- Multiparity
- Menopause
- Coc use
- Smoking

Symptoms

- Asymptomatic (75%)
- Heavy menstrual bleeding
- Dysmenorrhea
- Pelvic pain
- Abdominal mass
- Difficulty inmituration
- Constipation
- Infertility

Degenerative changes in fibroid:

AVOID RED HOT FATTY MEAT OF CHICKEN (MNEMONIC)

A – Atrophy

R- Red degeneration

H- Hyaline degeneration

F- Fatty degeneration or calcification

M- Myxomatous degeneration

C- Cystic degeneration

Investigations

- Cbc/ Hb
- Usg
- Saline infusion sonography
- Hysteroscopy - best to detect small submucous fibroid
- Laparoscopy
- MRI

Management

- Small [<5cm] with no pain / no bleeding / no infertility – **No Rx required**
- Small [<5cm] with pain / no bleeding / no infertility – **Rx required**
- Large [>10cm] – **Rx required**
- Large [>10cm] with no pain / no bleeding / no infertility – **Rx required**

Management is of two types

- Medical
- Surgical

Medical management

It is used to

- Decrease bleeding
- Decrease size

Drugs that bleeding / blood loss

- ✓ LNG
- ✓ IUCD
- ✓ OCP
- ✓ Tranexamic acid

Drugs that decrease the size of the fibroid

- ✓ Ullipristone
- ✓ Aromatase 1 inhibitor – Letrozole
- ✓ Gnrh agonist
- ✓ Gnrh antagonist
- ✓ Mifepristone
- ✓ Danazol/ gestrinone

INDICATION OF SURGICAL MANAGEMENT

- Menorrhagia
- Chronic pelvic pain with severe dysmenorrhea
- Unexplained infertility
- Recurrent abortion due to submucous fibroid
- Rapidly growing fibroid

SPECIFIC INDICATION FOR HYSTERECTOMY

- In patients >40 yrs of age
- Multiparous women
- If fibroid is associated with malignancy
- During myomectomy or surgical difficulty

Surgical management

Myomectomy – in younger women

Hysterectomy – in older women

FIGO CLASSIFICATION

SUBMUCOSAL

0 – Peduneuclated intracavity
1 - <50% intramural
2 - >50 % intramural

Other

3 contacts endometrium 100% intramural
4 Intramural
5 Subserosal
6 Subserosal <50% intramural
7 Subserosal peduneuculated
8 Other

Complication

- Degeneration
- Necrosis
- Infection
- Sarcomatous changes
- Hemorrhage
- Polycythemia
- Sarcoma

RED DEGENERATION OF FIBROID

- It is mostly seen during pregnancy especially in 2nd trimester
- It is aseptic condition
- It may become acutely painful enlarged & tender

Pathogenesis

As there is aseptic thrombosis in the blood vessels which supply the fibroid leading to subacute necrosis of fibroid

C/F

- Acute abdominal pain
- Vomiting
- Malaise
- Slight fever (not due to fever because of reactionary)

Pathological changes

- Fibroid because soft , necrotic or homogeneous especially into center
- It is stained salmon pink or red (due to diffusion of blood pigments from vessels)
- It has fishy odor

Diagnosis

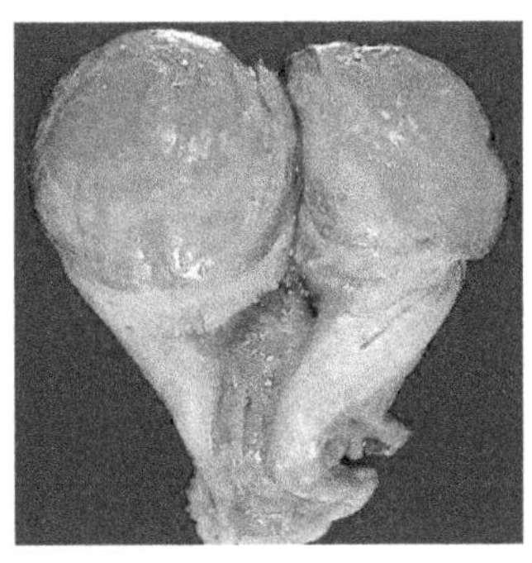

- Usg
- Esr will be elevated

Management

- ✓ Conservative management
- ✓ Analgesics
- ✓ Antipyretics
- ✓ Antiemetics

PALM- COEIN CLASSIFICATION

AUB-P (polyp) AUB-A (adenomyosis) AUB-L (leiomyoma) AUB-M (malignancy and hyperplasia)	AUB-C (coagulopathy) AUB-O (ovulatory disorders) AUB-I (iatrogenic) AUB-E (endometrial) AUB-N (not yet classified)

ADENOMYOSIS

Benign ingrowing of endometrium into the myometrium.

Pathophysiology -

Endometrium tissue will shift to other place.

Most commonly – myometrium

- Ovary
- Myometrium

WHY ??? Because of multiple pregnancy construction & relaxation continuously occur so cell shift from its original position / location to other .

Clinical feature

- Menorrhagia
- Dysmenorrhea
- Abdominal cramp

Diagnosis

- USG
- MRI
- Per Vaginal examination

Treatment

- Antifibrolytic drug – Tranexamic acid
- Nsaid
- Muscle relxant
    - Hyosine
    - Dicyclomine
- IUDS
- Hormones (progesterone)

ENDOMETRIOSIS

The presence of endometrial tissue outside the uterine cavity .

Site :

- Abdominal
- Extra abdominal
- Umbilicus
- Lungs
- Pleura
- Ureter
- Kidney
- Legs

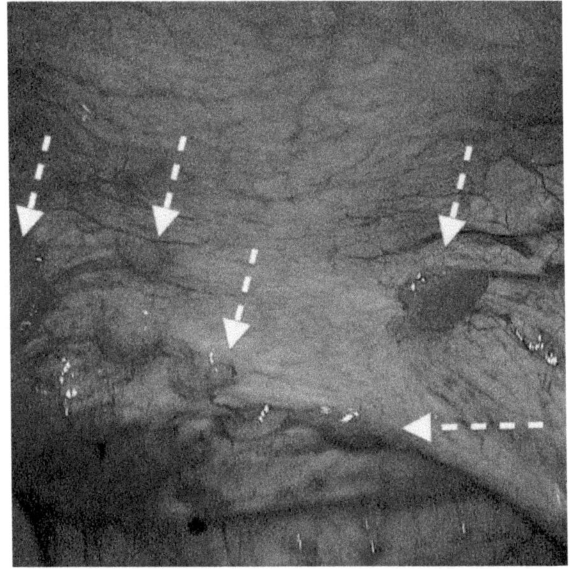

Most common sites

- Ovaries
- Pelvic peritoneum
- Pouch of douglas
- Uterosacral ligaments
- Sigmoid colon
- Appendix
- Fallopian tube

Risk factors

- Low parity
- Early menarche
- Late menarche
- Nulliparity
- Heavy alcohol & caffine consumption
- Obesity
- genital outflow obstruction
- Family history
- Prolonged 2nd stage of labor

Protective factor

- Regular exercise
- Smoking
- Pregnancy
- Multiparity

CHOCOLATE CYST

Endometrial blood deposit in the ovary so there is change in color of ovary known as chocolate cyst ovary .

Symptoms

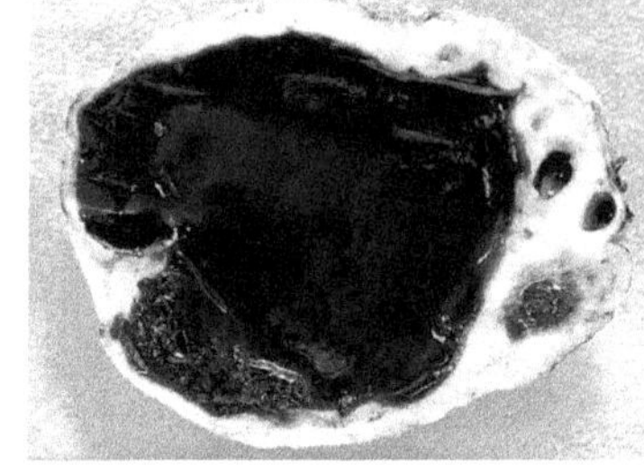

- Chronic pain
- Severe congestive dysmenorrhea
- Painful intercourse
- Menorrhagia
- Infertility

Investigations

- TVS – Chocolate cyst gives ground glass appearance
- Laparoscopy
- Histopathological examination
- CA-125

Treatment

- Surgical
    - Cystectomy – for chocolate cyst.
    - Adhesiolysis
- Medical management
    - NSAIDS
    - OCPs
    - Gnrh analogs
    - Danazol & Mifepristone

DERMOID CYST

It is also known as Benign cystic teratoma.

- Germ cell tumor

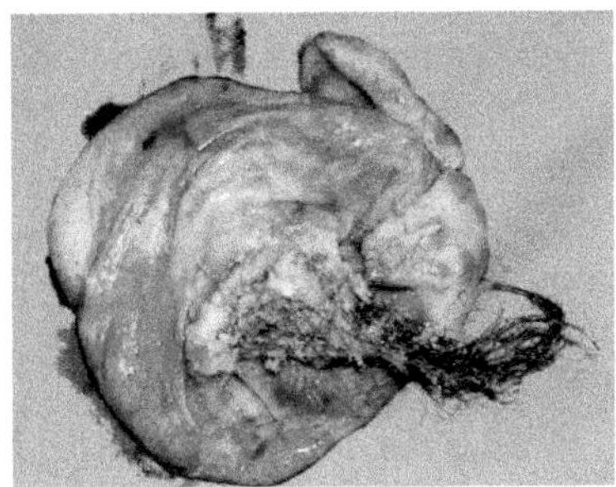

Symptoms.

- Pain
- Swellings
- Bleedings
- Constipation
- Painful urination
- Leg weakness

Diagnosis

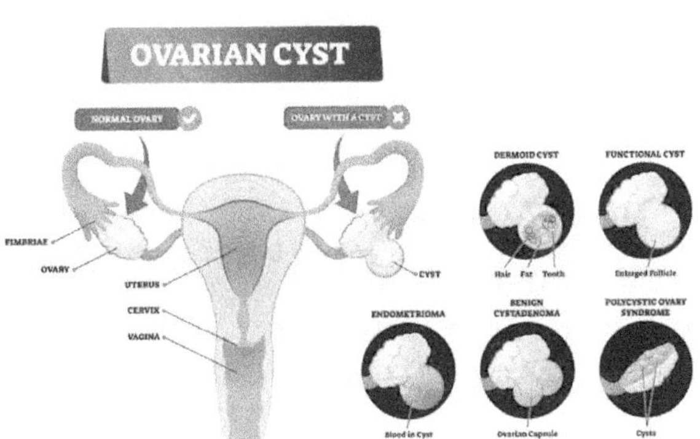

- Sonography
- CT scan
- MRI
- Serum Tumor
- Alpha fetoprotein
- Beta – HCG
- Cyst aspiration

Treatment

- ✓ Ovary cystectomy
- ✓ Ovariotomy

BARTHOLIN'S CYST

The Bartholin's glands are located on each side of the vaginal opening. These glands secrete fluid that helps lubricate the vagina.

Sometimes the openings of these glands become obstructed, causing fluid to back up into the gland. The result is relatively painless swelling called a Bartholin's cyst. If the fluid within the cyst becomes infected, you may develop a collection of pus surrounded by inflamed tissue (abscess).

A Bartholin's cyst or abscess is common. Treatment of a Bartholin's cyst depends on the size of the cyst, how painful the cyst is and whether the cyst is infected.

Symptoms

- A tender, painful lump near the vaginal opening
- Discomfort while walking or sitting
- Pain during intercourse
- Fever

Causes

Cause of a Bartholin's cyst is a backup of fluid. Fluid may accumulate when the opening of the gland (duct) becomes obstructed, perhaps caused by infection or injury.

A Bartholin's cyst can become infected, forming an abscess. A number of bacteria may cause the infection, including Escherichia coli (E. coli) and bacteria that cause sexually transmitted infections such as gonorrhea and chlamydia.

TREATMENT

Rest is imposed. Pain is relieved by analgesics and daily sitz bath. Systemic antibiotic—ampicillin 500 mg orally 8 hourly or tetracycline in chlamydial infection is effective. Abscess should be drained at the earliest opportunity before it bursts spontaneously. In case of recurrent Bartholin's abscess, excision should be done in the quiescent phase after the infection is controlled.

Marsupialization is the gratifying surgery for Bartholin's cyst. An incision is made on the inner aspect of the labium minus just outside the hymenal ring. The incision includes the vaginal wall and the cyst wall. The cut margins of the either side are to be trimmed off to make the opening an elliptical shape and of about 1 cm in diameter. The edges of the vaginal and cyst wall are sutured by interrupted catgut, thus leaving behind a clean circular opening.

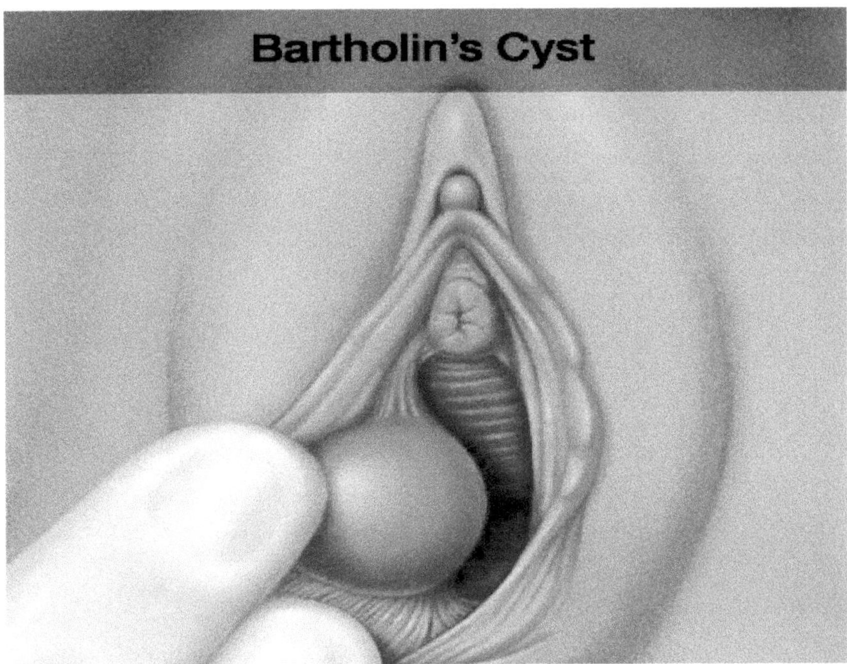

CHAPTER - 7

MALIGNANT LESIONS

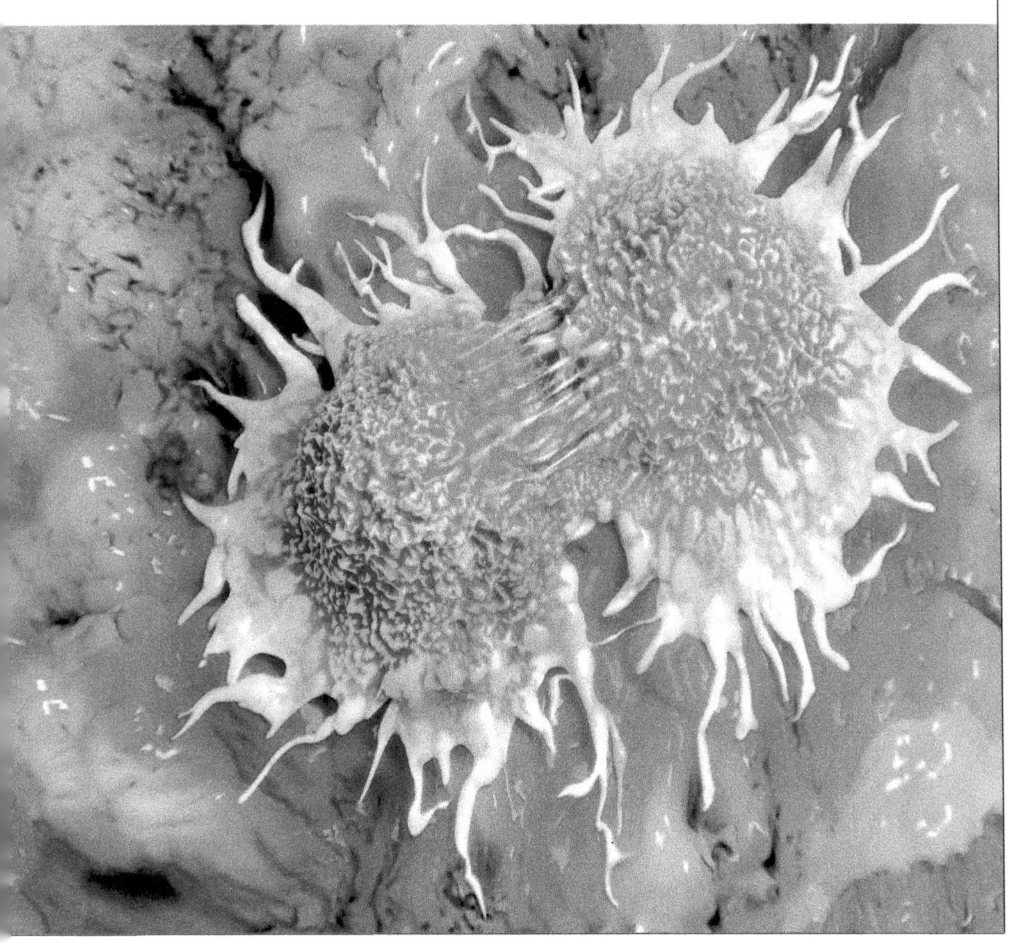

CERVICAL CARCINOMA

It is the most common cause of cancer of women in India

Etiology

- HPV 16 (Most common)
- HPV 18 (Most malignant)
- HIV 1&2
- HSV
- Commercial sex worker
- Women with multiple sex partner
- Early intercourse <16 yrs
- Smokers
- Ocp users
- Low socio economic status

Screening

PAP SMEAR

1. - By Iyer's spatula
    - Done only from anterior part of cervix
    - Sensivity – 47% to 62%
2. By cyto brush
    - Sensivity 90 % .

Site –Transformation Zone (squamo columnar junction)

- Endometrium – columnar
- Vagina &cervix – Squamous

Time to do Pap smear

- Any women more than 21 yr of age
- Any women 3 yrs after 1st sexual exposure
- If negative then do yearly
- More than 65 yrs no more pap smear is required if 10smear is negative after menopause .

Dysplasia Classification

CIN 1 – 1/3RD Abnormal
CIN II - 1/3RD – 2/3RD Abnormal
CIN III - > 2/3RD Abnormal
CIS – All cell are abomormal

CIN I ----**5 Yrs** ----- → CIN II -------- **10 Yrs** -------→ CIN III

Symptoms

- Deep pelvic pain
- Post coital bleeding
- Foul smelling discharge
- Pyometra

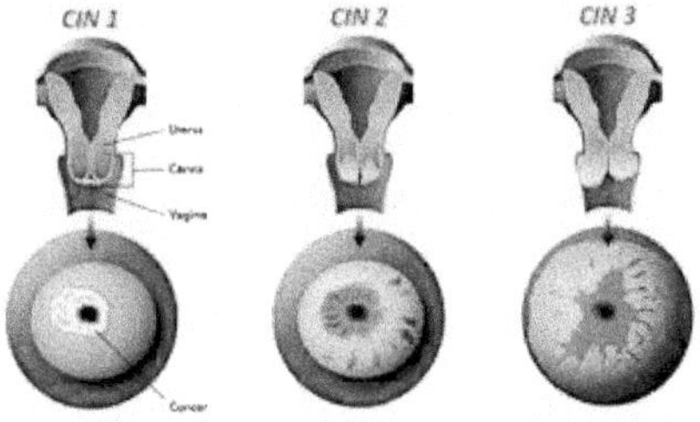

Signs

- Hardness
- Fixation
- Bleeds on touch

Revised FIGO staging of cervical carcinoma (2018)

- FIGO no longer includes stage 0 (Tis)
- **I:** confined to cervix uteri (extension to the corpus should be disregarded)
  - **IA:** invasive carcinoma only diagnosed by microscopy
    - **IA1:** stromal invasion <3 mm in depth
    - **IA2:** stromal invasion ≥3 mm and <5 mm in depth
  - **IB:** invasive carcinoma with measured deepest invasion ≥5 mm (greater than stage IA), lesion limited to the cervix uteri
    - **IB1:** invasive carcinoma ≥5 mm depth of stromal invasion and <2 cm in greatest dimension
    - **IB2:** invasive carcinoma ≥2 cm and <4 cm in greatest dimension
    - **IB3:** invasive carcinoma ≥4 cm in greatest dimension
- **II:** beyond the uterus, but has not extended onto the lower third of the vagina or to the pelvic wall

- **IIA:** involvement limited to the upper 2/3 of vagina without parametrial invasion
    - **IIA1:** invasive carcinoma <4 cm in greatest dimension
    - **IIA2:** invasive carcinoma ≥4 cm in greatest dimension
- **IIB:** with parametrial involvement but not up to the pelvic wall

- **III:** carcinoma involves the lower third of the vagina and/or extends to the pelvic wall and/or causes hydronephrosis or non-functioning kidney and/or involves pelvic and/or paraaortic lymph nodes
  - **IIIA:** carcinoma involves the lower third of the vagina, with no extension to the pelvic wall
  - **IIIB:** extension to the pelvic wall and/or hydronephrosis or non-functioning kidney (unless known to be due to another cause)
  - **IIIC:** involvement of pelvic and/or para-aortic lymph nodes, irrespective of tumor size and extent
    - **IIIC1:** pelvic lymph node metastasis only
    - **IIIC2:** para-aortic lymph node metastasis
    - with r (imaging) and p (pathology) notations to indicate how lymph nodes were identified
- **IV:** carcinoma has extended beyond the true pelvis or has involved (biopsy-proven) the mucosa of the bladder or rectum (bullous edema, as such, does not permit a case to be allotted to stage IV)
  - **IVA:** spread to adjacent organs
  - **IVB:** spread to distant organs

MOST COMMON PRESENTATION OF CA CERVIX IN INDIA IS **IIIB**

TNM Staging 2021

Primary tumor (T)

- **Tx**: primary tumor cannot be assessed
- **T0**: no evidence of primary tumor
- **Tis**: carcinoma in situ (cis)
- **T1**: cervical carcinoma confined to the uterus (extension to the corpus should be disregarded)

- **T1a**: invasive carcinoma diagnosed only by microscopy (depth of invasion < 5 mm)[11]
- **T1b**: clinically visible lesion confined to the cervix

- **T2**: cervical carcinoma invades beyond uterus but not to pelvic wall or to lower third of vagina
  - **T2a**: tumor without parametrial invasion
  - **T2b**: tumor with parametrial invasion
- **T3**: tumor extends to pelvic wall and/or involves lower third of vagina, and/or causes hydronephrosis
  - **T3a**: tumor involves lower third of vagina, no extension to pelvic wall
  - **T3b**: tumor extends to pelvic wall and/or causes hydronephrosis or nonfunctioning kidney (unless known to be due to another cause)
- **T4**: tumor invades the mucosa of bladder or rectum, and/or extends beyond true pelvis [11]

Regional lymph nodes (N)

- **Nx**: regional lymph nodes cannot be assessed
- **N0**: no regional lymph nodes metastasis
- **N1**: regional lymph node metastases to pelvic lymph nodes only
- **N2**: regional lymph node metastasis to para-aortic lymph nodes, with or without positive pelvic lymph nodes [11]

Distant metastasis (M)

- **M0**: no distant metastasis
- **M1**: distant metastasis (includes metastasis to inguinal lymph nodes, intraperitoneal disease, lung, liver, or bone; excludes metastasis to pelvic or para-aortic lymph nodes or vagina)

ALL CANCER IN GYNECOLOGY ARE STAGED SURGICALLY EXCEPT CA CERVIX WHICH IS STAGED CLINICALLY

MANAGEMENT

Stage I – IIA - RADICAL HYSTERECTOMY

Stage IIB or > IIB – CHEMORADIATION

Anticancer Drug Used – **CISPLATIN**

MAXIMUM RADIATION GIVEN AT

Point A – 2cm above & 2cm lateral to external os

- **Upto 7500 To 8000 Rads Given**

Point B – 3cm lateral to point A

- **Upto 6000 Rads are given**

VACCINES

- **GUARDASIL –** Quadrivalent HPV-6,11,16,18
- **CERVARIX –** Bivalent HPV- 16,18

THESE VACCINES ARE GIVEN AFTER 9 YEARS OF AGE UPTO 25 YRS

ENDOMETRIAL CARCINOMA

ETIOLOGY

- Estrogen
- Tamoxifen intake
- An-ovulatory conditions – PCOD
- Estrogen producing ovarian cancer
- Early menarche
- Late menopause
- Ca - breast
- Ca - endometrium
- Ca – ovary
- Nulliparous women

TYPES

- TYPE -1 Oestrogen dependent
- TYPE -2 Oestrogen Independent

- **Type I** are oestrogen-dependent and account for 90% growths. The source of oestrogen may be endogenous or exogenous. They are well-differentiated with good prognosis.
- **Type II** are oestrogen-independent and develop in atropic endometrium. They are mostly undifferentiated with poor prognosis. P_3 mutations are recognized in type II tumours.

CLINICAL FEATURES

- Post menopausal bleeding
- Pyometra
- Irregular acyclical bleeding

INVESTIGATIONS

- ✓ Pap smear
- ✓ Aspiration cytology
- ✓ Fractional curettage
- ✓ Hysteroscopy & Biopsy
- ✓ Ultrasound
- ✓ Doppler usg
- ✓ CA125 tumour marker
- ✓ Ct scan
- ✓ MRI
- ✓ X-Ray
- ✓ Pet ct gold standard for staging

FIGO SURGICAL STAGING OF ENDOMETRIAL CARCINOMA (2009)

Stage I	Tumour confined to the corpus uteri
IA	No or less than half myometrial invasion
IB	Invasion equal to or more than half of the myometrium
Stage II	Tumour invades cervical stoma, but does not extend beyond the uterus**
Stage III	Local and/or regional spread of the tumour
IIIA	Tumour invades the serosa of the corpus uteri and/or adnexae#
IIIB	Vaginal and/or parametrial involvement#
IIIC	Metastases to pelvic and/or para-aortic lymph nodes#
IIIC1	Positive pelvic nodes
IIIC2	Positive para-aortic lymph nodes with or without positive pelvic lymph nodes
Stage IV	Tumour invades bladder and/or bowel mucosa, and/or distant metastases
IVA	Tumour invasion of bladder and/or bowel mucosa
IVB	Distant metastases, including intra-abdominal metastases and/or inguinal lymph nodes

TREATMENT

STAGE I & II

- Grade I – Myometrium < ½ involved – Nothing required
- Grade II - Myometrium > ½ involved – Vaginal irradiation
- Grade III – Pelvic Irradiation

Cervical involved – Whole Abdomen Irradiation

STAGE III & IV

- Radiotherapy
- Surgical therapy
- Chemotherapy
- Hormonal therapy

CYTOTOXIC AGENTS WHICH CAN BE USED ARE AS FOLLOWS

- CISPLATIN
- CARBOPLATIN
- CYCLOPHOSPHAMIDE
- ADRIAMYCIN
- PROGESTOGENS
- TAMOXIFEN

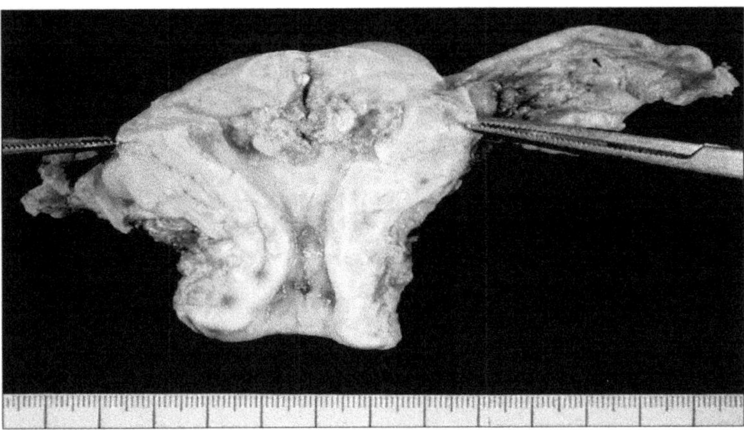

EPITHELIAL OVARIAN CANCER (EOC)

Definitions

• EOC is derived from surface epithelium of ovary. Incid: 12.8/100000 women/y

• 5th leading cause of cancer death in US. 90% of all ovarian cancers.

• Lifetime risk: 1.5%. Risk of death: 1%.

• Presentation red flag sx: Incidental abdominal pain, abdominal distension, loss of appetite, rectal bleeding, postmenopausal bleeding, weight loss.

Pathology

• **Serous tumors:** Low & high grade

• 40–50% of EOC; most common type of EOC. 60% bilateral. Psammoma bodies seen in low-grade tumors. Most common in BRCA carriers & in pts w/ Lynch syn

• Mucinous tumors (*Int J Gynecol Cancer* 2008;18:209)

• 10% of EOC. 8–10% bilateral

• Endometrioid adenoCa

• 10% of all ovarian cancers. 28% bilateral. 42% a/w endometriosis; 15–20% a/w endometrial carcinoma

• Clear cell cystadenocarcinoma

• 10% of all ovarian cancers. 40% bilateral. A/w endometriosis & HyperCa.

• Brenner/transitional cell carcinoma

• Rare, poorly differentiated similar to high-grade transitional cell carcinoma of bladder

• Carcinosarcoma

• 1–4% of all ovarian neoplasms. Carcinomatous & sarcomatous elements. Often stage III or stage IV at dx. Poor overall survival.

• Metastatic tumors

• **Krukenberg tumor:** Signet ring cell, GI tumor. Colonic adenoCa. Pancr adenoCa.

Breast cancer: Accounts for 6–40% of metastatic tumors to ovary; often bilateral.

Renal cell carcinoma. Burkitt's lymphoma. Low malig potential (borderline) tumor:

Mucinous or serous.

Risk factors:

- ✓ Nulliparity
- ✓ Early menarche
- ✓ Late menopause
- ✓ White race
- ✓ Increasing age
- ✓ Personal h/o breast cancer.

Protective factors:

- ✓ Long-term OCP use
- ✓ Tubal ligation
- ✓ Hysterectomy
- ✓ Breastfeeding

Lifetime risk with mutation : 28–44%; higher w/ BRCA1. Cancer occurs 10 y earlier

Symptoms

- Bloating – Abdominal distension, Discomfort
- Loss of appetite
- Increase frequency of maturation
- Sudden weight loss
- Irregular menses

Investigation

- ✓ Serum Ca125
- ✓ Human epididymis protein
- ✓ CBC , RBS, RFT , LFT, HIV, ECG
- ✓ CHEST-XRAY
- ✓ USG
- ✓ CT SCAN
- ✓ MRI
- ✓ FNAC & BIOPSY

FIGO CLASSIFICATION

STAGE 1: Tumour is confined to the ovary/ovaries.

1A	Only one ovary is affected by the tumour, the ovary capsule is intact
	No tumour is detected on the surface of the ovary
	Malignant cells are not detected in ascites or peritoneal washings
1B	Both ovaries are affected by the tumour, the ovary capsule is intact
	No tumour is detected on the surface of the ovaries
	Malignant cells are not detected in ascites or peritoneal washings
1C	The tumour is limited to one or both ovaries, with any of the following:
	The ovary capsule is ruptured
	The tumour is detected on the ovary surface
	Positive malignant cells are detected in the ascites or peritoneal washings

STAGE 2: Tumour involves one or both ovaries and has extended into the pelvis.

2A	The tumour has extended and/or implanted into the uterus and/or the fallopian tubes
	Malignant cells are not detected in ascites or peritoneal washings
2B	The tumour has extended to another organ in the pelvis
	Malignant cells are not detected in ascites or peritoneal washings
2C	Tumours are as defined in 2A/B, and malignant cells are detected in the ascites or peritoneal washings

STAGE 3: The tumour involves one or both ovaries with microscopically confirmed peritoneal metastasis outside the pelvis and/or regional lymph node metastasis.

Includes liver capsule metastasis.

3A	Microscopic peritoneal metastasis beyond the pelvis

3B	**Microscopic peritoneal metastasis beyond the pelvis 2 cm or less in greatest dimension**
3C	**Microscopic peritoneal metastasis beyond the pelvis more than 2 cm in greatest dimension and/or regional lymph nodes metastasis**

STAGE 4: Distant metastasis beyond the peritoneal cavity. Liver parenchymal metastasis.

Treatment

- For all 1-4 Stage ,The main treatment consist of staging laparotomy , primary cytoreductive surgery followed by chemotherapy.

Primary cytoreductive surgery -

- Total abdominal hysterectomy
- Bilateral salpingo oophorectomy
- Lymph node dissection

Conservative surgery –

- Unilateral salpingo oophorectomy

Chemotherapy

- Cisplatin
- Carboplatin
- Docetaxel

Prevention

Factor reducing the risk of ovarian cancer

- Ocp uses
- Breast feeding
- Multiparity
- Pregnancy

DYSGERMINOMA

It is the most common malignant germ cell tumor of ovary , it corresponds to the seminoma of the testis.

Etiology / Risk factors

- Genetic
- Turner syndrome
- klinefelter syndrome

Symptoms

- Abdominal enlargement
- Presence of mass in lower abdomen
- Abdominal pain
- Weight loss

Gross features

- Variable size
- Solid , fleshy tumor,with smooth exterior
- Capsulated
- Firm consistency
- Cystic degeneration
- Necrosis

Diagnosis

- Ct Scan
- MRI
- USG

Treatment

- Blcomycin 15mg IV / IM
- ETOPOSIDE100mg
- Cisplatin 20mg

- Vincristine
- Adriamycin
- Cyclophosphamide

KRUKENBURG TUMOR

It is a metastatic malignancy of ovary characterized by mucin rich signet ring adenocarcinoma.

Etiology

- Gastric and colorectal cancer

Symptoms

- Abdominal mass
- Abdominal pain
- Pain with intercourse
- Bloating
- Weight loss
- Abnormal vaginal bleeding

Treatment

- Chemotherapy
- Radiotherapy

CHAPTER - 8

CONTRACEPTION & INFERTILITY

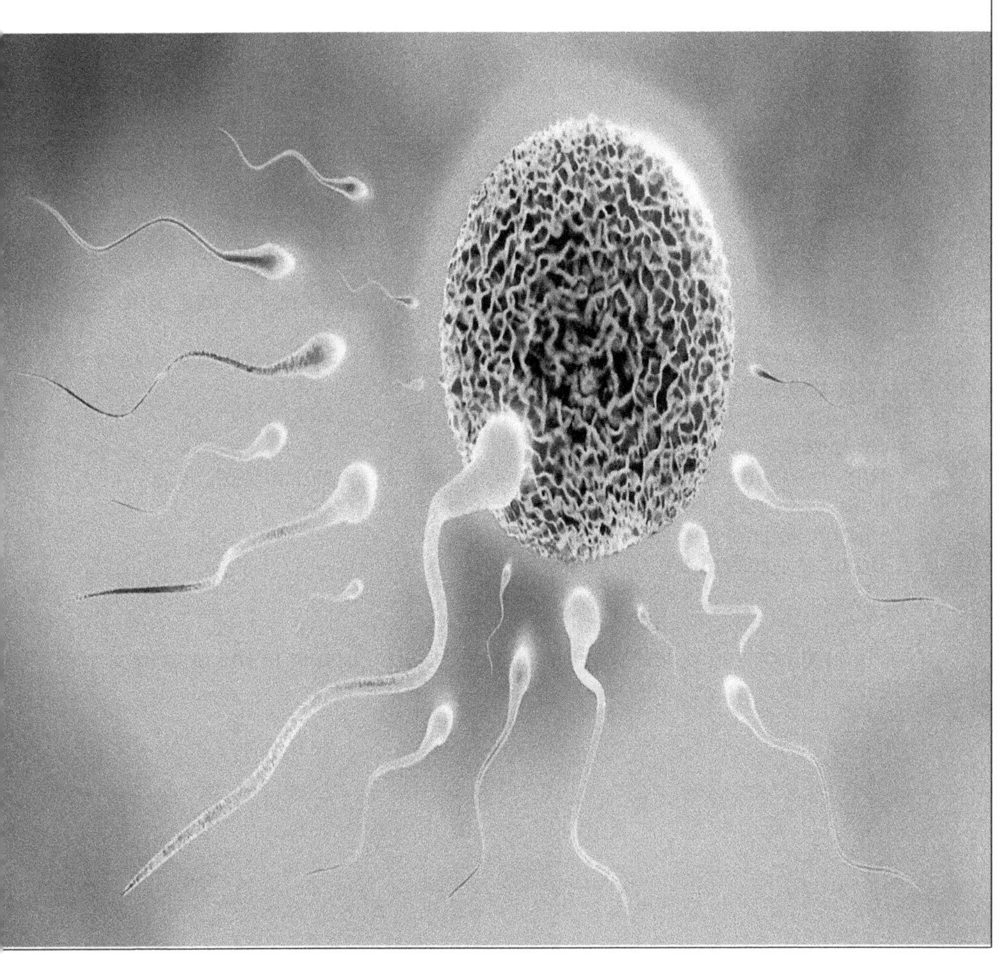

Contraception is defined as the intentional prevention of conception through the use of various devices, sexual practices, chemicals, drugs, or surgical procedures. Thus, any device or act whose purpose is to prevent a woman from becoming pregnant can be considered as a contraceptive.

The choice of contraception depends upon the following:

- Availability, cost.
- Age and parity of the couple.
- Reliability (failure rate).
- Side effects, contraindications to a particular method.
- Advantages and disadvantages

Methods of Contraception

1. Natural methods:
   - Abstinence during the fertile phase.
   - Withdrawal (coitus interruptus).
   - Breastfeeding.
2. Barrier contraceptives:
   - Use of condoms by male.
   - Use of spermicidal agents.
   - Use of diaphragm, or the cervical cap in the vagina, use of female condom.
   - Use of hormones which alter the cervical mucus and prevent entry of sperms into the cervical canal.
3. Intrauterine contraceptive devices (IUCDs).
4. Suppression of spermatogenesis.
5. Suppression of ovulation with hormones—hormonal contraceptives.
6. Interceptive agents (postcoital contraception).
7. Immunological methods.
8. Surgical sterilization

Pearl index

Failure rate of any contraceptive method is described in terms of pregnancy rate per 100 woman years.

NATURAL METHODS

The methods of contraception described in this section—periodic abstinence, coitus interruptus, and lactational amenorrhea—are physiology-based methods that use neither chemical nor mechanical barriers to contraception. Many couples, for religious, philosophical, or medical reasons, prefer these methods to other forms of contraception. However, these are the least effective methods of contraception and should not be used if pregnancy prevention is a high priority.

PERIODIC ABSTINENCE

THE RHYTHM METHOD ('Safe Period') The woman must take her temperature every morning and watch out for the sustained rise which indicates ovulation. Women with regular periods ca often usually identify the periovulatory time with a fair degree of accuracy. However, an episode of hormonal irregularity may occur without warning and this can put the woman at risk of pregnancy. However, assuming the cycle is regular and lasts for 28 days, ovulation usually occurs between the 12th and 14th days of the cycle. 24 h are allowed for ovum survival and 3 days should be allowed as survival time of the sperms in the genital tract, although sperm have been shown to survive for up to a week. This means that intercourse must be avoided from the 9th to the 15th day and a 24 h safety margin at either end increases the avoidance period from the 8th to the 17th day, both inclusive..

Effectiveness

The average effectiveness of periodic abstinence is relatively low (55% to 80%) compared with other forms of pregnancy prevention.

Advantages and Disadvantages

Periodic abstinence uses neither chemical nor mechanical barriers to conception and is, therefore, the method of choice for many couples for various reasons. However, this method requires a highly motivated couple willing to learn reproductive physiology, predict ovulation, and abstain from intercourse. Periodic abstinence is relatively unreliable compared with the more traditional methods of contraception. This low reliability may require prolonged periods of abstinence and regular menstrual cycles, making it less desirable for some couples.

COITUS INTERRUPTUS

Method of Action

Coitus interruptus, or withdrawal of the penis from the vagina before ejaculation, is one of the oldest methods of contraception. With this method, the majority of semen is deposited outside of the female reproductive tract with the intent of preventing fertilization.

Effectiveness

The failure rate for coitus interruptus is quite high (27%) compared with other forms of contraception. Failure can be attributed to the deposition of semen (pre-ejaculate) into the vagina before orgasm or the deposition of semen near the introitus after intracrural intercourse.

Advantages and Disadvantages

The primary disadvantage of coitus interruptus is its high failure rate. Other disadvantages include the need for sufficient self-control to withdraw the penis before ejaculation.

LACTATIONAL AMENORRHEA

Method of Action

Continuation of breastfeeding has long been a widespread method of contraception for many couples. After delivery, the restoration of ovulation is delayed because of a breastfeeding-induced hypothalamic suppression of ovulation. Specifically, there is a prolactin-induced inhibition of pulsatile gonadotropin-releasing hormone (GnRH) from the hypothalamus resulting in suppression of ovulation.

Effectiveness

The duration of ovulatory suppression during breastfeeding is highly variable. In fact, 50% of lactating mothers will begin to ovulate between 6 and 12 months after delivery, even while breastfeeding. Importantly, returnof ovulation occurs before the return of menstruation. As a result, 15% to 55% of mothers using lactation for contraception subsequently become pregnant. The effectiveness of lactational amenorrhea as a short-term method of contraception can be enhanced by following certain principles. First, breastfeeding should be the only form of nutrition for the infant. Second, this method of contraception should be used only as long as the woman is experiencing amenorrhea and, even then, it should only be used for a maximum of 6 months after delivery. Following these guidelines, lactational amenorrhea as a method of contraception can have a much lower failure rate. In practice, however, most mothers are not able to meet these stringent requirements.

Advantages and Disadvantages

Lactational amenorrhea has no effect on breastfeeding and is safe, simple, convenient, and free. Studies show that babies who receive breast milk have increased body contact and bonding, have a lower risk of infections, and benefit from exposure to maternal antibodies. The use of lactational amenorrhea is limited to the immediate 6 months after delivery and can result in vaginal dryness for some women. Also, while the theoretical failure rates are reasonable, the failure rates for actual practice are so high as to make this an unacceptable and unreliable sole means of contraception.

BARRIER METHODS AND SPERMICIDES

MALE CONDOMS

Method of Action

Condoms are latex sheaths placed over the erect penis before ejaculation. They prevent the ejaculate from being released into the reproductive tract of the woman.

Effectiveness

When properly used, the condom can be 98% effective in preventing conception. The actual efficacy rate in the population is 85% to 90%. To maximize effectiveness and decrease the risk of condom breakage, it is important to leave a well at the tip of the condom to collect the ejaculate and to avoid leakage of semen as the penis is withdrawn. Efficacy is also increased by use of spermicide-containing condoms or by using a spermicide along with condoms.

Side Effects

Some individuals may experience a hypersensitivity to the latex, lubricant, or spermicide in condoms.

Advantages and Disadvantages

Condoms are widely available for a moderate cost and carry the added benefit of preventing the transmission of many sexually transmitted infections (STIs). Condoms are the only method of contraception that offers protection against human immunodeficiency virus (HIV). Drawbacks of the male condom include coital interruption and possible decreased sensation or hypersensitivity.

FEMALE CONDOMS

Method of Action

The female condom; also known as an internal condom, is a pouch made of synthetic nitrile (previously polyurethane) that has a flexible ring at each end. One ring is silicon based and lubricated. It is inserted into the depth of the vagina, and the other ring stays outside the vagina near the introitus . The female condom may also be inserted into the anus.

Effectiveness

The theoretical failure rate of the female condom is 5%. However, studies show that the actual failure rate of the female condom is 20% to 25%, somewhat higher than that of the male condom. However, these were short term studies and may not reflect the failure rate with long-term usage.

Advantages and Disadvantages

By covering the vagina or anus, female condoms protect against STIs, while also placing the control of contraception with the female partner. Efforts are underway to develop a latex female condom and to make the female condom more accessible in developing countries. The female condom is also hormone free and relatively easy to obtain without a prescription. Because of its design, it will stay in place even if the male erection is lost. Major drawbacks include cost and overall bulkiness. Some users report decreased sensation during intercourse. The nitrile and lubricant may also cause irritation of the penis, vagina, anus, or vulva. The acceptability rating is somewhat higher for the male partner (75% to 80%) than for the female partner (65% to 70%).

DIAPHRAGM

Method of Action

The vaginal diaphragm is a dome-shaped shallow cup made of a soft silicone or latex (rubber) sheet which is stretched over a thin coiled rim. Spermicidal gel, foam or cream is placed on the rim and on either side of the diaphragm, and it is placed into the vagina, so that it covers the cervix. The diaphragm and spermicide should be placed in the vagina before intercourse and left in place for a minimum of 6 hours (maximum of 30 hours) after intercourse. If further intercourse is to take place within 6 to 8 hours after the first episode of intercourse, additional spermicide should be placed in the vagina without removing the diaphragm.

Effectiveness

The theoretical effectiveness of the diaphragm approaches 94%. The actual effectiveness rate of the diaphragm with spermicide is 80% to 85%.

Side Effects

Possible side effects include bladder irritation, which can lead to urinary tract infections. If the diaphragm is left in place too long, colonization by *Staphylococcus aureus* may lead to the development of **toxic shock syndrome**. Some women also experience a hypersensitivity to the rubber, latex, or spermicide.

SPERMICIDES

Method of Action

Spermicidal agents come in varying forms, including vaginal creams, gels, films, suppositories, and foams. The most widely used spermicides are nonoxynol-9 and octoxynol-9. Other agents, such as menfegol and benzalkonium chloride, are used .Nonoxynol-9 and octoxynol-9 both disrupt the cell membranes of the spermatozoa and also act as a mechanical barrier to the cervical canal. In general, spermicides should be placed in the vagina at least 30 minutes before intercourse to allow for dispersion throughout the vagina. Spermicides may be used alone but are far more effective when used in conjunction with condoms, cervical caps, diaphragms, or other contraceptive methods.

Effectiveness

When properly and consistently used with condoms, spermicides can have an effectiveness rate as high as 95%. However, in actual usage, the efficacy of spermicides when used alone is only 70% to 75%. This effectiveness is further reduced by failure to wait long enough for the spermicide to disperse in the vagina prior to intercourse.

Side Effects

Spermicides can irritate the vaginal mucosa and external male and female genitalia.

Advantages and Disadvantages

Spermicidal agents are widely available in a variety of forms and are relatively inexpensive. Some formulations can also be messy to use. In addition to providing contraception, it was initially thought that spermicides might provide some protection against STIs. However, it now appears that these agents do not confer any protection against STIs. They may, in fact, make the user more susceptible to STIs, including HIV by causing vaginal irritation. For this reason, spermicides should not be used by women with HIV or at high risk of contracting HIV. This is of special significance in developing nations where contraception and STI prevention are paramount. For the general public, it is strongly recommended that consistent condom use be employed whenever protection against STIs is desired.

INTRAUTERINE DEVICE IUDS

Intrauterine device (IUD) is a small, flexible plastic frame to be inserted into the uterine cavity.

Inert or non-medicated

These devices are made of plastic or stainless steel only. Lippes loop made of plastic (polyethylene) impregnated with barium sulphate is still used in many parts of the world. Stainless steel rings are widely used in China only.

Copper IUDs

Copper wire or copper sleeves are put on the plastic frame (polyethylene frame). Examples include Copper T, CuT380 A, Multiload 375 etc.

The various types of Copper IUDs differ from each other by the amount of copper. The initial Copper IUDs were wound with 200-250 mm2 wire (CopperT 200). The modern copper containing devices contain more copper and a part of copper in the form of solid tubal sleeves rather than wire. This increases the efficacy and lifespan (Cu T-380 A).

- ***CuT 380A*** - It is a T shaped device with a polyethylene frame holding 380 mm2 of exposed surface area of copper. The IUD frame contains barium sulfate thus making it radio-opaque.

- ***CuT-380Ag*** - It is identical to 380 A except that the copper wire on the stem has a silver core to prevent fragmentation and extend the life span of the copper.

- ***CuT 380 slimline*** - It has copper sleeves flushed at the ends of horizontal arms to facilitate easier loading and insertion. The performance of CuT-380 Ag and the CuT-380 slimline is equal to that of CuT-380 A.

- ***Multiload 375*** - It has 375 mm2 of copper wire wound around its stem. The flexible arms are designed to minimize expulsions. The multiload 375 and T cu-380 A are similar in their efficacy and performance.

- ***Nova T*** - It is similar to the CuT-200, containing 200 mm2 of copper. However, the Nova T has a silver core to the copper wire, flexible arms, and a large flexible loop at the bottom to prevent cervical perforation.

Hormone-Releasing IUDs

- ***Progestasert*** - It is a T shaped IUD made of ethylene and vinyl acetate copolymer containing titanium dioxide. The vertical stem contains a reservoir of 38 mg progesterone together with barium sulfate dispersed in silicone fluid. The progesterone is released at the rate of 65 µg per day.

• ***LNG - 20 (Mirena)*** **-** This T shape & device has a collar attached to vertical arm containing 52 mg of levonorgestrel dispersed in poly dimethyl siloxane. It releases 15µg of levonorgestrel per day in vivo and is effective for 7-10 years.

Mechanism of action

IUD mainly work by changing the intra-uterine environment and making it spermicidal. Non-medicated IUD cause a sterile inflammatory response by producing a tissue injury of minor degree but sufficient enough to be spermicidal.

Copper containing IUD, in addition, release free copper and copper salts that have both a biochemical and morphological impact on the endometrium and also produce alteration in cervical mucus and endometrial secretions. No measurable increase in serum copper is observed.

Hormone releasing IUD add progesterone effect on endometrium to the foreign body reaction. The endometrium becomes decidualized with atrophy of glands. The progesterone IUD does not increase the serum progesterone level and mainly acts by inhibition of implantation, sperm-capacitation and survival. Levonorgestrel IUD produces serum concentrations of the progestin half those of Norplant and therefore, ovarian follicular development and ovulation is not inhibited. The LNG-20 IUD decreases the blood loss (by about 40-50%) and dysmenorrhoea.

Contraindications

- Pregnancy
- Puerperal sepsis or immediate post septic abortion
- Distorted uterine cavity (congenital or acquired)
- Unexplained vaginal bleeding
- Suspected genital malignancy
- High-risk candidate for sti
- Genital tuberculosis
- Active pelvic inflammatory disease (pid)

Specific contraindications to LNG-20 IUD

- Current deep vein thrombosis/pulmonary embolism
- Current or past history of ischaemic heart disease

- Migraine with focal neurological symptoms (at any age)
- Current and past history of breast cancer
- Active viral hepatitis, cirrhosis of liver and benign or malignant liver tumors

Timing of Insertion

After childbirth

- immediately after delivery of placenta (post-placental insertion)
- four to six weeks after childbirth

After spontaneous or induced abortion

- immediately after 1st trimester abortion (aseptic).
- after 2nd trimester abortion it is advisable to wait till involution of uterus is complete.

Menstrual cycle

- can be inserted any time, during menstrual cycle, if reasonably sure that woman is not pregnant and has not been having sex without contraception.
- insertion during menstruation offeres following advantages :

– pregnancy is ruled out

– insertion is easier due to open cervical canal

– any minor bleeding caused by insertion is less likely to upset the client

SIDE EFFECTS

- Perforation
- PID
- Dysmenorrhoea (2–10%)
- Vaginal infection
- Actinomycosis

ORAL CONTRACEPTIVE PILLS (OCPs)

Types of Oral Contraception

A. Hormonal

B. Non-hormonal

A. Hormonal: There are two main categories of hormonal contraceptives:

- Combined hormonal contraceptives contain both an estrogen (usually ethinyl estradiol) and a progestin
- Progestin-only contraceptives contain only progesterone a synthetic analogue (progestin).

Combined Oral Contraceptive (COC) - Taken daily, irrespective of intercourse. Releases a low dose of both estrogen and progestin into the bloodstream. Effectiveness depends on regular intake.

- ✓ Monophasic
- ✓ Biphasic
- ✓ Triphasic

Progestin-Only Pill (POP) -.The progestogen-only pill (POP) is ideal for women who like the convenience of pill taking but wish to avoid COC. It is taken every day without a break. Although the failure rate of the POP is greater than that of COC , it is ideal for women at times of lower fertility as detailed below. If the POP fails, there is a slightly higher risk of ectopic pregnancy.

Releases a low dose progestin into the bloodstream. Effectiveness depends on regular intake at the same time every day (within a window of 3 hours). Safe for breastfeeding women.

Levonorgestrel Emergency Contraceptive Pill (ECP) - A progestin-only method. Prevents pregnancy in emergency situation (unprotected /accidental intercourse) to be taken within 72 hours as a single dose (1.5 mg). Emergency contraceptive pills do not provide ongoing protection against pregnancy.

Types of monophasic combined oral pills

1st generation	Ethinyl oestradiol	Norethindrone
2nd generation	Ethinyl oestradiol	Norgestrel, LNG
3rd generation	Ethinyl oestradiol	Desogestrel, gestodene norgestimate
4th generation (Yasmin)	Ethinyl oestradiol	Drospirenone

Subdermal implant

There was a need to explore the other routes of progestogen delivery into general circulation with slow, sustained release, long-acting and with reduced side effects. The subdermal implant has no 'nuisance value' of continuous compliance which often adversely affects motivation. Besides, nonoral system avoids 'hepatic first pass effect and systemic side effects'. To reduce the frequent visits to the clinics, ensure an even release of the hormone and reduce the side effects while maintaining the efficacy; implants containing various amounts of progestogen have been used subdermally. **Norplant I** containing six silastic capsules has been withdrawn and replaced by a single rod implant.

Norplant II (Jadelle) consists of two rods each containing 70 mg LNG. The daily release of hormone is 50 mcg and provides contraception for 3–5 years. The implants suppress ovulation in 50% but the main action is suppressing endometrium. The implants are inserted on the first day of the menstrual cycle, within 5 days of abortion, and 3 weeks after the delivery. The woman needs to use barrier contraception or abstain in the first 7 days of insertion. It takes 5–10 min to insert under local anaesthesia. It is best inserted on the medial aspect of the upper arm. Since the capsules are nonbiodegradable, they need removal at the end of its use or earlier, if side effects are intolerable. The insertion and removal is made easier by using a single rod, Implanon (40 3 2 mm), which contains 67 mg desogestrel and does not require an incision to insert. It elutes 30 mcg of the hormone daily and the effect lasts 3 years. There has been no failure to date. It prevents ovulation and is reversible within 1 month of removal. Implanon—Amenorrhoea is common at the end of

Advantages.

- The advantages of implants are:
- They are long-acting with sustained effect—compliance is good.
- Coital-independent with no 'nuisance' of daily oral or frequent injections.
- Pregnancy rate—varies between 0.2 and 1.3 per 100 woman years. The failure rate is higher in obese women weighing more than 70-kg.
- Systemic side effects are few and first pass effect on the liver avoided.
- Return of fertility has been mentioned.
- Can be used by lactating mothers and over the age 40.

Disadvantages

- Breakthrough bleeding, irregular cycles, amenorrhoea occur as with other progestogenic contraceptives.
- Other side effects of progestogens exist.
- Ectopic pregnancy is reported in 1.3%.
- Local infection may occur.
- Requires insertion and removal with nonbiodegradable capsules, which are however minor surgical procedures.
- Failure rate (pregnancy) has been mentioned above.
- The implants are expensive and cost Rupee 10,000.
- Infertility is seen in a few cases.

B. Non-Hormonal: Centchroman (Ormeloxifene)

A non-steroidal, non-hormonal method, taken twice a week on fixed days for the first three months, followed by once a week thereafter. Safe for breastfeeding women.

PERMANENT STERLIZATION

Male Sterilization Vasectomy

Vasectomy consists of dividing the vas deferens and disrupting the passage of sperms. It is done through a small incision in the scrotum, under local anaesthesia. The sterility is not immediate. The sperms are stored in the reproductive tract for up to 3 months. The couple must therefore abstain from intercourse during this period or use other methods of contraception. Approximately, 20 ejaculates clear the semen of all sperms. Two semen analysis reports must confirm the absence of sperms before the man can be declared sterile. No-scalpel technique has been now adopted. One single incision is made with a special forceps and skin stitch is not required. Clips and plugs can be applied over the vas instead of cutting. Vasectomy is cheaper than tubectomy

Complications of Vasectomy:

- Local pain, skin discolouration, bleeding, haematoma formation (1–2%).
- Infection (1%), trauma to the testicular artery causing gangrene, rare.
- Antibody formation and autoimmune disease (40%).
- Failure rate of 0.15/100 woman years at the end of 1 year.
- Granuloma formation in 0.1–3% cases.
- Spontaneous recanalization.
- Formation of spermatocele.
- Decreased libido or impotency are mainly psychological in origin and occur in men who were not properly motivated.
- Does not prevent HIV, STD.

Advantages

- It is an outpatient procedure.
- Local anaesthesia is adequate.
- It is a minor surgical procedure and the man can resume duty after rest of 1 or 2 days.
- Libido not affected. No evidence of prostate cancer

Female Sterilization Tubectomy

A few small incisions are made around the belly button. A telescopic device known as a laparoscope is inserted through one of the cuts. There is a small camera at the tip of the laparoscope which transmits images to a screen, providing the surgeon with a view of the internal organs. Guided by the images and working through the tiny cuts, the surgeon inserts special instruments to seal the tubes by cutting parts of them or by blocking them using clips.

Types

- Bipolar coagulation- Electric current is used to sear parts of the fallopian tubes.
- Monopolar coagulation- The tubes are seared using electric current. A radiating current is also used to further damage them.
- Tubal clip- The fallopian tubes are blocked by permanently clipping them or tying them together.
- Tubal Ring- The tube is tied using a silastic band.
- Fimbriectomy- In this procedure, a section of the fallopian tube is disconnected from the ovary. This creates a gap, hampering the capacity of the tube to receive eggs and transfer them to the uterus.

INFERTILITY

It is defined as an inability to conceive after 12 months of unprotected intercourse.

Types

Primary infertility is a condition where a couple, who have had no previous pregnancies, are unable to conceive.

Secondary infertility is a condition where a couple, who have had at least one previous pregnancy that may have ended in a livebirth, stillbirth, miscarriage, ectopic pregnancy or induced abortion, are unable to conceive.

Aetiology

Lifestyle factors such as heavy smoking or being significantly over- or underweight and stress can adversely affect both male and female fertility.

Cause

- Female 40-55%
- Male 40%
- Unexplained

CAUSES OF FEMALE FACTOR INFERTILITY

- With increasing age, women become less fertile.
- There are many causes of infertility (see below). Sometimes, failure to conceive can be due to a combination of factors. However, in approximately 30% of cases, a clear cause is never established.

Unexplained infertility 28%

- Male factor infertility 21%
- Ovulatory disorders 18%
- Tubal disease 14%

- Endometriosis 6%
- Coital problems 5%
- Cervical factors 3%

Other factors that may play a part include chronic medical conditions such as diabetes, epilepsy and thyroid and bowel diseases.

CAUSES OF MALE FACTOR INFERTILITY

Infertility is often thought of as a female issue, but in around 30% of cases, it is because of a problem in the male partner. As in women, male fertility is also thought to decline with age, although to what extent is unclear. Possible causes of male infertility include:

- ✓ Problems with the tubes carrying sperm
- ✓ Erectile dysfunction
- ✓ Ejaculatory problems
- ✓ Previous orchitis
- ✓ A past bacterial infection that caused scarring and blocked tubes within the epididymis as it joins the vas
- ✓ Past medical treatment such as drug treatment, radiotherapy or surgery – for example, to correct a hernia, undescended testes or twisted testicles
- ✓ Genetic problems
- ✓ Chronic diseases such as diabetes
- ✓ Drugs.

INVESTIGATIONS IN THE PRIMARY SETTING

When a couple presents to their general practitioner with the issue of infertility, these initial investigations should be carried out.

Female partner

- Cervical smear test.
- Urine test for Chlamydia (this can cause blockages of the fallopian tube).
- Serum progesterone level to check ovulation. This is taken 1 week prior to menstruation, hence day 21 for a 28-day cycle or day 28 for a 35-day cycle

- Rubella immunity – if rubella is contracted during the first 3 months of pregnancy it can seriously harm the developing fetus Women who are not immune to rubella should be vaccinated, and advised to avoid pregnancy for 3 months.
- Measuring serum FSH (follicle stimulating hormone), LH (luteinizing hormone) and oestradiol to identify hormone imbalances or possible early menopause.

Male partner

- Semen analysis to check for abnormalities of the sperm such as number, motility, and morphology.
- Urine test for Chlamydia, which, in addition to being a known cause of infertility in women, can also affect sperm function and male fertility.

INVESTIGATIONS IN THE SECONDARY SETTING

These are done in the context of a tertiary fertility clinic and after the primary investigations have been carried out. Some or all of the following tests will be done.

Female partner

- Measuring serum FSH, LH and oestradiol to identify hormone imbalances or possible early menopause.
- Serum progesterone level to check ovulation. This is taken 1 week prior to menstruation, hence day 21 for a 28-day cycle or day 28 for a 35-day cycle.
- A pelvic ultrasound scan to look at uterine and ovarian anatomy.
- Serial ultrasound tracking of the ovaries for looking at developing follicles.
- Checking of tubal patency – either by hysterosalpingogram, hysteron-contrast sonography or laparoscopic hydrotubation.
- Diagnostic laparoscopy – to check for problems with tubal and uterine anatomy.
- Hysteroscopy – to check for uterine conditions such as fibroids or polyps
- Endometrial biopsy (in rare cases)

Male partner

- Sperm antibody test to check for protein molecules that may prevent sperm from fertilising an egg.

FEATURES SUGGESTIVE OF OVULATION

1. Clinical symptoms and signs

Regular menstruation is usually associated with ovulation, however, no clinical symptoms or signs are sufficiently reliable to confirm ovulation. Supportive laboratory tests are always required.

2. Changes in basal body temperature

The secretion of progesterone by the corpus luteum induces a rise of around 0.5 °C in basal body temperature (BBT). If BBT is recorded throughout the menstrual cycle, a fall in temperature is often observed at the time of the LH surge. Charts typical of those generated by

A) A woman with a normal ovulatory cycle

B) A woman with an anovulatory cycle,

The differences in BBT between ovulatory and anovulatory women are not sufficiently consistent for a diagnosis of ovulation to be made without further tests.

TESTS THAT CONFIRM THE OCCURRENCE OF OVULATION

1. Serum progesterone levels

Estimation of serum progesterone is a simple method for confirming ovulation.Progesterone is produced by the corpus luteum and its levels reach a peak in the midluteal phase (i.e. 7 days prior to menstruation). If the measured serum progesterone levels are low, this may indicate either that the patient is not ovulating, or that the blood sample was withdrawn at an inappropriate time in the cycle. Information about the time of the subsequent menstrual period is required to accurately interpret the relevance of serum progesterone levels.

2. Endometrial biopsy

The presence of a secretory endometrium confirms that ovulation has taken place. Under the influence of progesterone, the endometrial glands dilate, and secretory vacuoles may be observed within the glandular cells. If an endometrial biopsy is taken in the luteal phase and examined histologically, secretory changes can be observed. A biopsy of the endometrium is a relatively invasive process, but it gives useful information, especially if sensitive progesterone assays are unavailable.

3. Serial ovarian ultrasound

Over the course of the menstrual cycle, an ovarian follicle develops, grows to 20 mm and the oocyte is then released at ovulation. This process can be visualised by a transvaginal ultrasound examination every 2–3 days during the follicular, ovulatory and early luteal phases. This procedure is too invasive and expensive to be used in an unselected population of women complaining of infertility. However, it is often used to monitor the number and size of the developing ovarian follicles in women undergoing ovulation induction. The serial ultrasound is the only method of detecting the luteinised unruptured follicle syndrome (LUF).

TESTS WHICH CONFIRM NORMAL SPERM PRODUCTION

Semen Analysis

A basic semen analysis assesses the number, morphology and motility of spermatozoa. The patient is asked to provide a sample (usually by masturbation), which should be analysed within 2 hours of production. The sample should be kept warm (15–38 _C) during the interval from production to analysis. Abstinence from sexual activity for a period of 2–3 days is required before submitting a sample for analysis; otherwise an abnormally low count may be recorded. The patient should also be advised to keep the sample away from spermicidal agents, such as those in condoms.

The criteria for normal spermatogenesis may vary from laboratory to laboratory. The WHO criteria are shown below:

1. Volume: 2 ml

2. Concentration: 20 million/ml

3. Motility: 50% with forward motility (within 60 min of ejaculation)

4. Morphology: 30% normal forms

5. White blood cells: <1 million/ml

TESTS OF TUBAL PATENCY

1. Laparoscopic hydrotubation

Tubal patency can be assessed at laparoscopy. A cannula is inserted into the cervix, and 5–20 ml of methylene blue dye is injected into the cavity of the uterus. If the fallopian tubes are patent, the dye can be seen spilling out of the end of each tube. An important advantage of laparoscopic hydrotubation is that it enables inspection of the pelvic organs during the procedure. Conditions such as pelvic adhesions and endometriosis, both of which may reduce fertility, can be noted. The major disadvantage of laparoscopy is that it is an operative procedure that requires a general anaesthetic.

2. Hysterosalpingography

Hysterosalpingography is the radiological visualisation of the genital tract after the injection of a radio-opaque contrast medium through the cervix. Hysterosalpingography may be a useful supplementary test in women who have tubal blockage that is demonstrated at laparoscopy. Hysterosalpingography allows the site of tubal blockage to be determined, which is helpful if surgery is contemplated.

3. Hysterosalpingo-contrast sonography.

Tubal patency can also be assessed by an ultrasound examination. A solution containing galactose microparticles, visible on ultrasound, is injected though the cervix. If the fallopian tubes are patent, the solution can be observed passing along the tubes and out through the fimbrial ends.

4. Falloposcopy

Advances in imaging techniques have allowed the manufacture of hysteroscopes that are small enough to be passed into the fallopian tube.

Internal tube morphology can be directly assessed. This procedure is only available in specialised centres, but it can be combined with operative treatments to relieve fallopian tube blockage.

ASSISTED REPRODUCTION TECHNIQUES

- ✓ The treatment of subfertility is very much dependent on the cause. Available techniques include:
- ✓ Fertility drugs
- ✓ In vitro fertilisation (IVF) with or without pre-implantation genetic diagnosis (PIGD)
- ✓ Intrauterine insemination (IUI)
- ✓ Donor insemination (DI)
- ✓ Intracytoplasmic sperm injection (ICSI)
- ✓ Gamete intrafallopian transfer (GIFT)
- ✓ In vitro-maturation (IVM)
- ✓ Reproductive immunology
- ✓ Surrogacy.

FERTILITY DRUGS

These are used for inducing ovulation. Some women may become pregnant with these drugs alone, or alternatively, these may be used in combination with other treatments such as IVF or IUI. Commonly used drugs include:

1. Clomiphene

Clomiphene is a non-steroidal antioestrogen. It has complex actions, including an oestrogen-agonistic activity at the endometrium. The major effect of clomiphene is at the hypothalamus, and it induces ovulation by increasing pituitary gonadotrophin production. Its side effects include hot flushes, mood swings, nausea, breast tenderness, insomnia, increased urination, heavy periods, spots and weight gain. The risk of ovarian cancer can also increase slightly if it is taken for over a year.

2. Metformin

This is an oral insulin sensitising medication that helps stimulate ovulation in women with the polycystic ovarian syndrome. Potential side effects of this drug include nausea, vomiting, diarrhoea, abdominal pain, a metallic taste, itching, allergic reactions and rarely hepatitis.

3. Gonadatrophin releasing hormone analogues

This is administered by a small pump, which injects pulses of the drug into the bloodstream. It is used mainly in ovulation failure caused by a lack of GnRH. Possible side effects include abdominal pain, nausea, vomiting, heavy periods and headaches.

4. Gonadotrophins

Follicle stimulating hormone (FSH), Gonal-f and Puregon Luteinising hormone (LH), such as Menogon, Menopur and Merional The use of gonadotrophins to induce ovulation should only be carried out in specialized centres. The patient should be monitored by ovarian ultrasound (to determine the number of follicles and their diameter) combined with serum or urinary oestrogen assays. These drugs are generally used before treatment cycles during assisted conception, or for polycystic ovary syndrome in which clomiphene has not been effective. They are administered as once-daily injections and act by stimulating follicle production in the ovaries. When the follicles are mature (as deemed by ovarian tracking), an injection of human chorionic gonadotrophin hormone (hCG) is given to trigger the release of an egg(s). Ovarian hyperstimulation syndrome (OHSS), risk of multiple pregnancies when used for ovulation induction, allergic reactions and skin reactions are the potential side effects.

5. Progesterone (Cyclogest, Gestone, Crinone, Progynova)

This is generally given after the hCG injection or on the day the embryos are returned to the womb. Its purpose is to prepare the endometrium for nurturing an embryo. This may help maintain the pregnancy after IVF or IUI.

6. Bromocriptine and carbergoline

These tablets reduce high levels of prolactin, which can be a cause of subfertility. Side effects include nausea, headache, constipation, dry mouth, skin reactions, hair loss and a lowering of the voice.

CHAPTER - 9

PROLAPSE

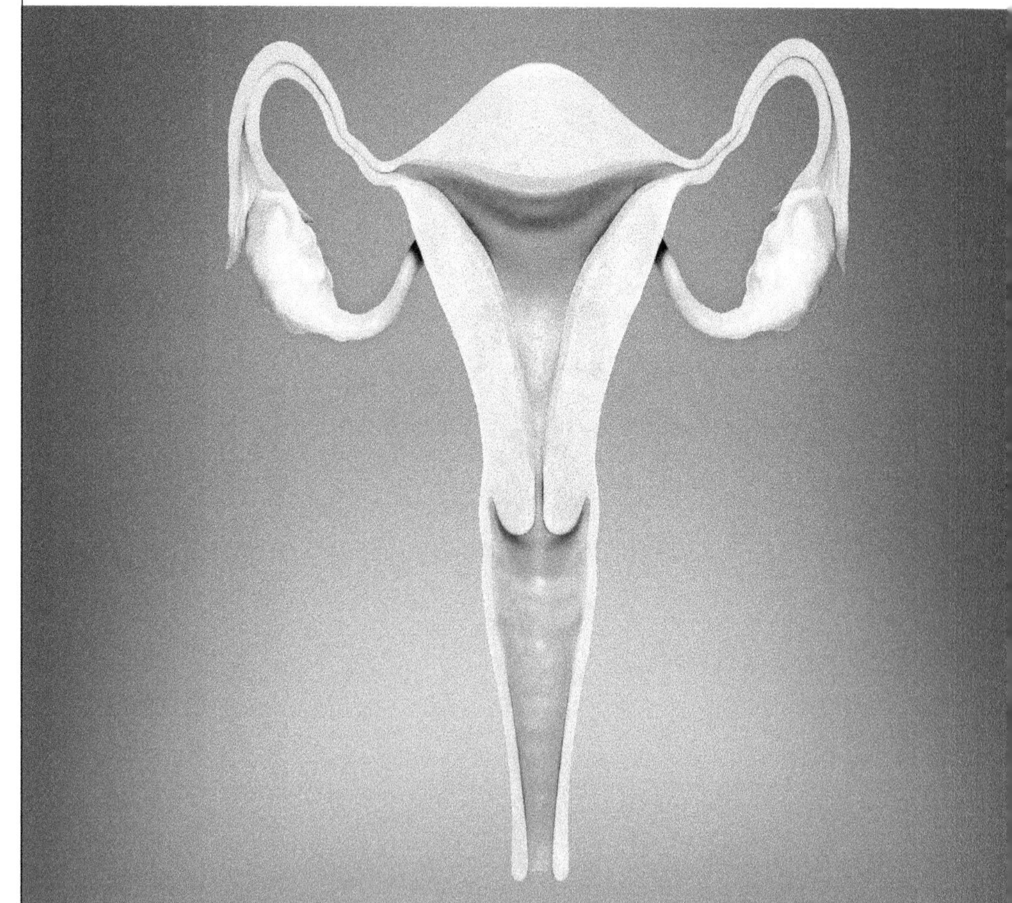

Protrusion of pelvic organ into or out of the vaginal canal is called prolapse.

ETIOLOGY

Acquired causes

- Weakened Supports
    - Repeated child birth
    - Menopause
- Traumatic deliveries
- Faulty birth practices
- Increased intra abdominal pressure

Congenital causes

- Spina bifida occulta
- Ehler danlor syndrome

SYMPTOMS

- Groin / back pain
- Feeling of heaviness
- Pain during sexual intercourse
- Incomplete evacuation
- Urgency of mituration

SHAW'S CLASSIFICATION

Stage 1 – cervix is just below the normal level

Stage 2 – cervix is at vaginal opening

Stage 3 – cervix is at outside the vafinal opening

Stage 4 – Procidentia

PART OF PROLAPSE [Anterior to Posterior]

- Anterior vaginal wall
- Urethrocele
- Cystocele
- Uterus
- Rectocele
- Posterior vaginal wall

COMPLICATION

- Infection
- Stone formation
- Retension of urine
- Decubitous ulcer

PREVENTION OF PROLAPSE AFTER DELIVERY

- Physiotherapy
  - Antenatal
  - Postnatal

TREATMENT

For Elderly women

- Vaginal Hysterectomy + Pelvic floor repair (also known as ward & mayor operation)

For younger women

- Fothergill's operation (Manchester repair)

for nulliparous prolapse of very ypung women

- Sling surgeries

CHAPTER - 9

ECTOPIC PREGNANCY

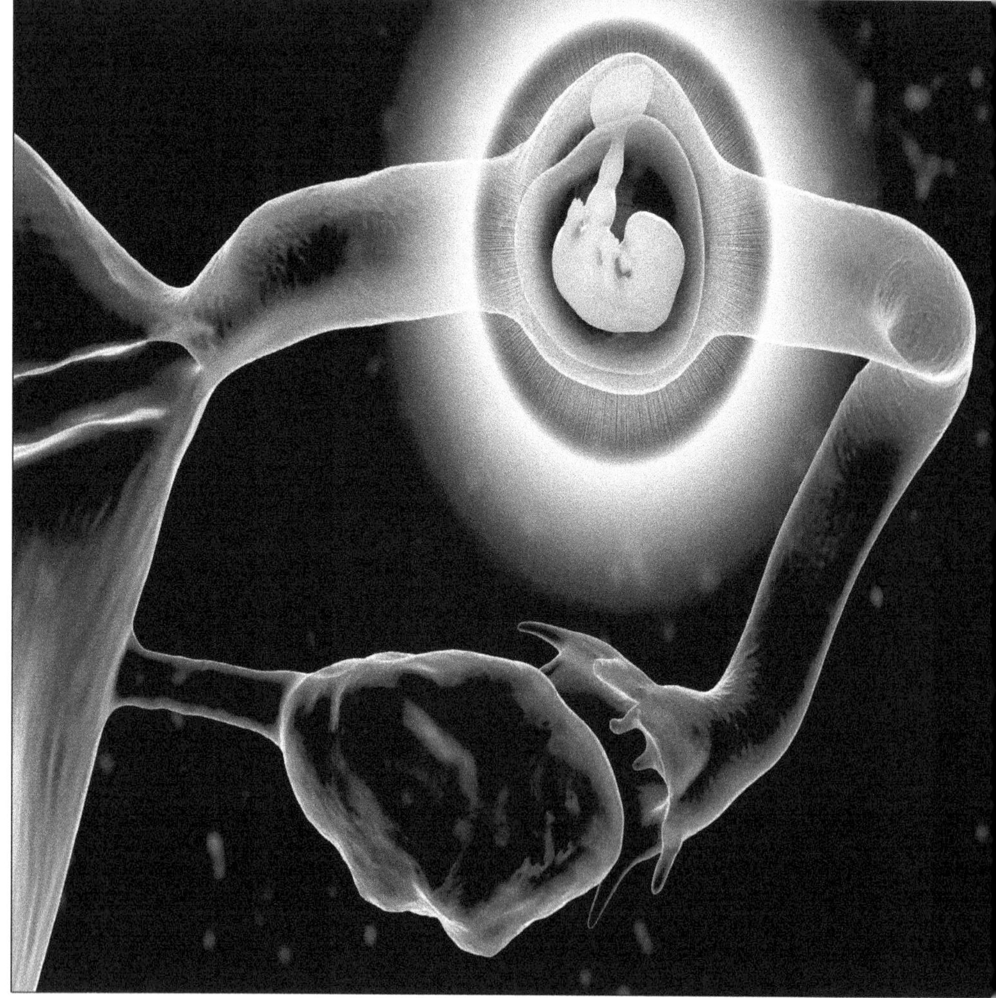

Implantation of pregnancy at a site other than endometrial lining in the body is called ectopic pregnancy .

TYPES

- Tubal
- Ovarian
- Abdominal
- Caesarean scar
- Cervical

AETIOLOGY

- Previous pelvic inflammatory disease
- Genital tuberculosis
- Endometriosis
- Previous ectopic pregnancy
- Previous tubal surgery
- Ivf program
- Progesterone only pill
- IUCD
- Smoking

SYMPTOMS

- Amenorrhea
- Pain abdomen
- Vaginla bleeding
- Retension of urine
- Fever

DIAGNOSIS

- Urinary / serum hcg
- B- hcg
- USG
- MRI
- Culdocentesis

MANAGMEMT

IF THE WOMEM IS HAEMODYNAMICALLY STABLE THEN

- Inj methotrexate 50mg IM

  Side Effects
  - Anemia
  - Leucopenia
  - Thrombocytopenia
  - Alopecia
  - Vomiting
  - Gastric haemorrhage

Other drugs which can be used are as follows

- Mifepristone
- Prostaglandins
- 20% KCL Solutions

But among all above methotrexate is most effective

if patient is haemodynamically unstable then laparotomy should be performed.

SURGICAL TREATMEMT

- Salpingectomy
- Partial salpingectomy
- Salpingostomy
- Milking of the tube

1. **What are the signs on physical examination of ectopic pregnancy ?**

Many women have a normal physical examination; however, the common signs are:

- Adenexal mass and/or tenderness
- Mild uterine enlargement
- Cervical motion tenderness
- Abdominal tenderness
- Orthostatic hypotension, tachycardia, and rebound tenderness are all signs of rupture

2. **What is the differential diagnosis of these symptoms?**

- Threatened abortion
- Torsion
- Ruptured corpus luteum cyst
- Abnormal uterine bleeding
- Tubo-ovarian abscess (TOA)
- Molar pregnancy
- PID
- UTI or stones
- Pyelonephritis
- Diverticulitis
- Appendicitis
- Pancreatitis

3. **What is the difference in b-hCG levels between an intrauterine and ectopic pregnancy?**

The rate of β-hCG rise is lower in most cases of ectopic pregnancy.

4. **What is a tubal abortion?**

The expulsion of the POC through the fimbria into the abdominal cavity. The POC can then either regress or reimplant in the abdominal cavity or in the ovary.

5. **What are the contraindications of methotrexate used to treat an ectopic Pregnancy ?**

- Active hemorrhage
- pregnancy larger than 4 cm
- Breastfeeding
- Alcoholism
- Peptic ulcer disease
- Liver or renal disease
- Blood dyscrasias

- Immunodeficiency
- Active pulmonary disease

6. **What are the two methods of methotrexate administration for the treatment of an ectopic pregnancy?**

- Give a single intramuscular (IM) dose of methotrexate and then follow β-hCG levels at days 4 and 7 hCG levels should decline by 15% between days 4 and 7.
- Alternate day IM administration of methotrexate until β-hCG level decreases by 15% in 48 hours .

7. **What are the differences between a salpingostomy and a salpingectomy?**

- Salpingostomy: an incision is made on the antimesenteric part of the fallopian tube and the POCs are evacuated. The incision is closed by secondary intention
- Salpingectomy: a tubal resection that involves partial removal of the oviduct, salvaging as much as possible.

8. **What is the difference in progesterone levels between an intrauterine and an ectopic pregnancy?**

Serum progesterone levels are lower in ectopic pregnancies compared with viable intrauterine pregnancies. However, the sensitivity and specificity of progesterone levels are too low to make it a screening or diagnostic test for ectopic pregnancy

CHAPTER - 10

VAGINAL DISCHARGE AND INFECTION

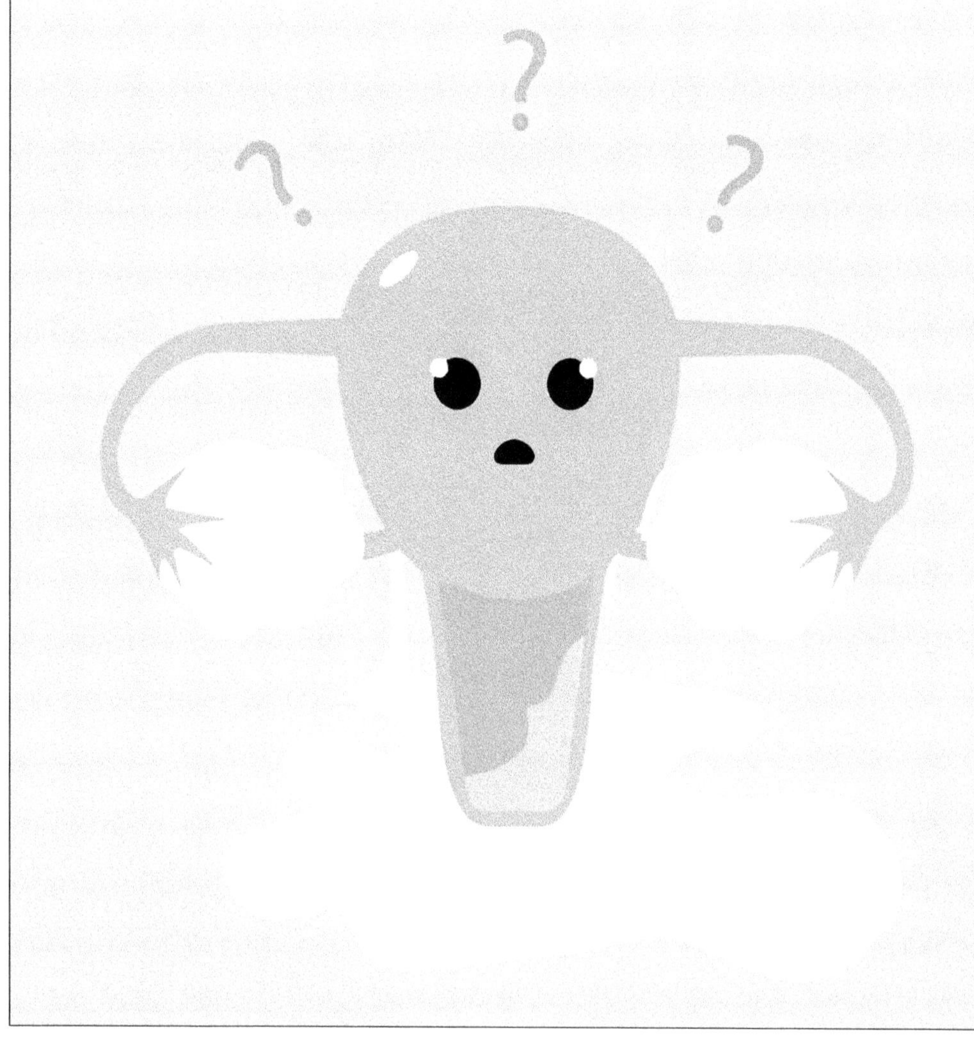

A small amount of vaginal discharge is normal in adult life and may be excessive in the presence of cervical ectopy. Cervical ectopy is where the glandular epithelium from the endocervix is visible on the ectocervix.

COMPOSITION

The vaginal discharge is composed of tissue fluid, cell debris, carbohydrate, lactobacilli and lactic acid. The pH is about 4.5, a degree of acidity that inhibits the growth of organisms other than the lactobacilli.

SOURCE OF VAGINAL DISCHARGE

Vulva: Greater vestibular glands, glands of vulval skin

Vagina: Mainly desquamated epithelial cells which liberate glycogen. The lactobacilli metabolise the glycogen to lactic acid. Vaginal transudate (secretion from tissues and capillaries of the mature vagina) is often described; vaginal epithelium is certainly not water resistant (like transitional epithelium). There are no mucosal glands.

Cervix: Alkaline mucous secretion which becomes copious and watery during ovulation.

Uterine glands also discharge into the vagina

CLINICAL FEATURES

Volume: The need to wear a pad or tampon continuously suggests excessive discharge.

Onset: Onset can be associated with the end of a pregnancy, the contraceptive pill, a course of antibiotic.

Colour: Normal discharge is white but stains yellow or pale brown on clothing or pads. A greenish-yellow colour suggests pyogenic infection, commonly accompanied by an unpleasant odour. Red or dark brown suggests blood.

Irritation: Any discharge can in time excoriate the vulva, but often Candida and Trichomonas cause itching.

LEUCORRHOEA

This means an excessive amount of normal discharge – a very subjective assessment. The patient will complain of constantly having to change her clothes but there will be no irritation and appearance will be normal. The smell will be the normal vulval odour (from the action of commensal bacteria on the secretions of the apocrine sex glands); microscopy will reveal normal appearances and culture will grow only lactobacilli. The patient should be reassured and given an explanation of normal physiology. No local treatment is necessary.

CANDIDA ALBICANS

This is yeast and exists in two forms – slender branching hyphae or as a small globular spore which multiplies by budding.

SOURCE OF INFECTION

This organism may exist as a normal commensal in the rectum and small numbers may be found in the vagina. Sexual transmission is also possible. Symptomatic infection is most likely to arise when there are predisposing conditions, examples of which are given below:

1. ***Pregnancy.*** The vagina provides a tropical microclimate and the high concentration of sex steroids in the blood maintains an increased glycogen formation in the vaginal epithelium and may alter the local pH.
2. ***Immunosuppressive therapy.*** This includes cytotoxic drugs and corticosteroids. There is also thought to be a natural degree of immunosuppression during pregnancy.
3. ***Glycosuria.*** This may be due to undiscovered diabetes, but again a mild degree of glycosuria may exist in a normal pregnancy because of the lowering of the renal threshold for sugar.
4. ***Antibiotic therapy.*** Systemic antibiotics destroy the normal bacteria, thus reducing the competition for nutrients, leaving the field clear for C. albicans.

CLINICAL FEATURES

The patient is usually between 20 and 40, when oestrogen support of the epithelial glycogen content is at its highest. The complaint is of irritant discharge and dyspareunia. Examination reveals an inflamed and tender vagina and vulva with white plaques resembling curdled milk adhering to the vaginal wall and vulva. Removal of the plaque reveals a red inflamed area. Pre-pubertal or postmenopausal infection is less common.

TREATMENT

A single 500 mg clotrimazole pessary, with external application of 1% clotrimazole cream, offers convenient therapy. Routine treatment of partners is unlikely to reduce recurrence rates. In persistent or recurrent infection, confirmation of the diagnosis by culture and determination of sensitivity to treatment are important. Oral antifungal medication can also be used

CHLAMYDIA TRACHOMATIS

This is a widespread gynaecological infection.

CLINICAL FEATURES

- The initial symptoms in women are often mild and may in fact be asymptomatic. Discharge may be present, varying from watery to frankly purulent according to the severity of the reaction to the disease. In severe cases, there is obvious cervicitis which looks like an infected erosion. Sometimes, there is a punctate haemorrhagic inflammation with microabscesses. Occasionally, there are few changes in the vagina and the first evidence of infection is the appearance of a salpingitis. It is an important cause of chronic pelvic inflammation. A gelatinous exudate is formed in the Pouch of Douglas which proceeds to multiple adhesions and tubal occlusion.

- It is an important cause of infertility. Ophthalmia neonatorum occurs if there is transmission to the neonate during delivery.
- Reiter's syndrome with urethritis, arthritis and conjunctivitis is more common in the infected male.
- It may spread to cause perihepatitis with so-called violin string adhesions to the parietal peritoneum. This is accompanied by acute pain in the upper right quadrant and is known as Fitz–Hugh–Curtis syndrome. It can be mistaken for cholecystitis or pancreatitis.

DIAGNOSIS

- Culture of Chlamydia requires sampling of endocervical cells, urethral cells or endosalpinx cells (salpingitis detected at surgery). They should be sent in special transport medium to an appropriate laboratory.
- Nucleic acid amplification techniques are now commonly used to diagnose chlamydia from a vulval swab or a first-void urine sample, with 30% greater sensitivity than viral culture.
- The organism can be seen under the microscope. It is intracellular. Staining by an immunofluorescence technique confirms the diagnosis. It multiplies like bacteria, but like viruses can only do so within cells. It contains both DNA and RNA.

TREATMENT

Azithromycin 1 g as a single dose or doxycycline 100 mg orally, twice a day for 7 days. Azithromycin and doxycycline are equally effective. The primary advantage of azithromycin is that it is administered in a single dose. Erythromycin should be given in pregnancy.

TRICHOMONAS VAGINALIS

- T. vaginalis is a protozoan organism, which infests the vagina in women and the urethra, prepuce and prostate in men. It is a common cause of irritant vaginal discharge.
- T. vaginalis is a single-cell organism about 20m x 10m, with four flagellae and an undulating membrane which gives it a characteristic jerky movement. It is transmitted mainly during sexual intercourse.

CLINICAL FEATURES

In the acute phase, the patient complains of severe vaginal tenderness and pain, and an irritant discharge. The vagina is seen to be inflamed, sometimes with a patchy strawberry vaginitis, and there is a copious, offensive, frothy discharge. Frequently there is a burning sensation, pruritus, dysuria and dyspareunia. In the latent or dormant phases, there are no symptoms although the presence of the organism can be demonstrated, often in a cervical smear.

PATHOLOGY

Passing from host to host during coitus, T. vaginalis attaches itself to the vaginal epithelium and multiplies rapidly, taking glycogen away from lactobacilli, which disappear. The vaginal pH rises to about 5.5, allowing the increase of bacterial pathogens that aggravate the infection and resulting discharge.

DIAGNOSIS

Diagnosis is by observation of the motile organisms in a fresh smear diluted with saline and by laboratory culture.

TREATMENT

Always systemic and, if possible, including the patient's sexual partner. Metronidazole (Flagyl) 400 mg thrice daily for a week, or 2 g orally once daily.

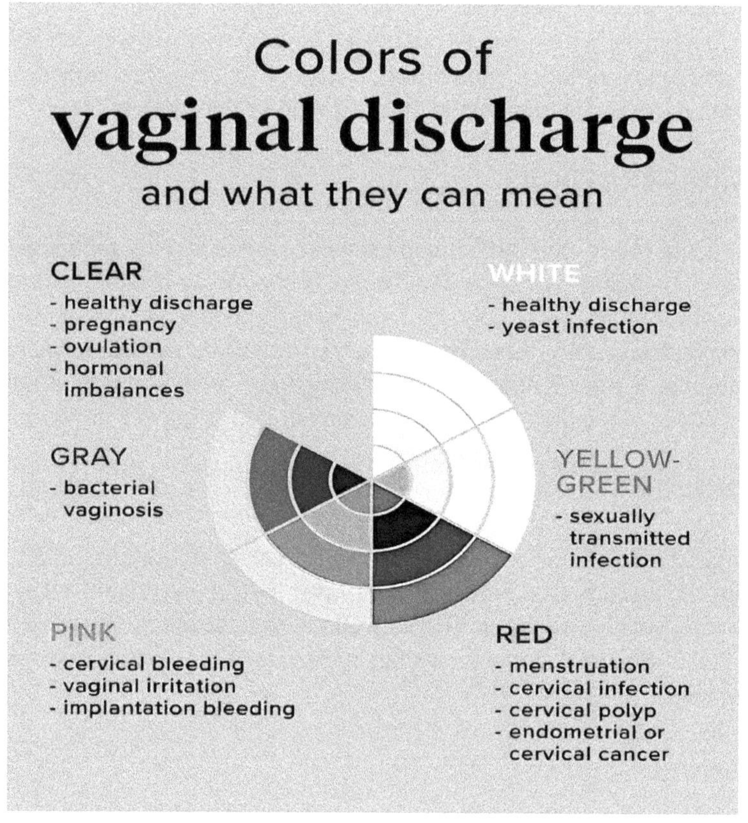

INDEX

www.ingramcontent.com/pod-product-compliance
Ingram Content Group UK Ltd.
Pitfield, Milton Keynes, MK11 3LW, UK
UKHW022018190726
13853UKWH00005B/1987